J.D. PLOETZ

NOTHING
CHANGES

When

NOTHING
CHANGES

UNIVERSAL BLUEPRINT FOR
MEANINGFUL CHANGE AND
LONG TERM SUCCESS

First edition
Printed in USA by Three Knolls Publishing, Tucson | 3knollspub.com

Dedication

This book is dedicated to all the technicians at A1 Garage Door Service—past, present, and future. Your dreams and dedication inspired this project and ultimately brought it to life.

Acknowledgments

A heartfelt thanks to Tommy Mello and Luke Martin for taking the time to offer your honest contributions. Your insights have only strengthened the need for a book like this.

I also want to express my gratitude to all my friends, family, and colleagues who read the manuscript and provided valuable feedback, even when I was convinced no changes were needed. Your honesty made this book better.

Preface

I'm writing this preface about 30 days after the book's completion. It's done—the cover is finished, and I could have uploaded it and started selling copies a month ago. But I was waiting on a couple of contributors whose input I had requested for certain parts of the book. So I waited, and that waiting turned out to be a learning experience— one where I had to practice exactly what I'm preaching in this book. I had to change the way I view *patience*, something I even dedicated an entire section to.

It's a bit ironic that writing the preface is usually one of the last steps in completing a book, especially since it comes first in the manuscript. To be honest, I had no idea what a preface really was before I started this process—this whole book-writing thing is new to me. But as I went through the journey of completing the book, I realized that the preface is where the real understanding of what the book is about comes together. It was news to me, but now it makes perfect sense.

Eventually, I received the contributions, sent them to the editor, and now we're a little behind schedule, but not by much. Honestly, it is what it is. The fact that the book is complete and ready to go is an accomplishment of immense proportions.

The extra time also allowed me to give out some advance copies to people for feedback, and the response has been overwhelmingly positive. Earlier today, I was talking to one of my technicians who read an advanced copy. He described the book as "Change 101." He said, "I understand how to evoke change, but you got me thinking from a completely different direction and gave me new tools to use—a guide to refer back to forever." Hearing that affirmed the purpose of this book.

The purpose of **Nothing Changes When Nothing Changes** is to get you, the reader, to a point where something you read, understand, or contemplate from this book triggers a desire to change something in your life. This change could lead to greater success, happiness, or any other positive outcome. My goal is that something in this book provides you with a new perspective, a tool, or a piece of knowledge that you didn't have before—something that compels you to take action and step out from where you are now.

This book is designed to be helpful to anyone. If you're advancing nicely in parts of your life and just need a fresh perspective to launch you into another level of change, it's here. If you're feeling stuck and don't know what to do next, it's for you as well. If you're in the middle of a crisis and need some direction to get you moving out of a situation, it's for you too.

This book is not only for those who have already navigated through numerous changes in life and found success but also for those who have struggled with change. It's for people who don't fully understand how change works, what mindset is needed, or how to give themselves every advantage to make a change stick. It's about getting back to the basics—being in the right frame of mind to want change, taking the necessary actions to create that change, following through, and ultimately achieving a positive transformation in your life.

Why did I write this book? After years in my current role, where I've asked my technicians to make positive changes, I noticed that some of them were simply unable to do so. Initially, I thought it was a lack of effort on their part. But the truth was, they didn't know *how* to change. So, I went through the very steps that are in this book with them—helping them understand the thinking needed to make successful changes. This process applies to any area of life, whether at work, in personal relationships, or any other aspect.

The reality is simple: *nothing changes when nothing changes*. If you're feeling stuck, stagnant, or unsure of how to move forward, know that there's something in your life that needs to change, and this book is here to help you figure out how to make that change. It's not that you don't want to change; it's that you may not know how.

I can't guarantee that every change you want to make will be successful just by reading this book. But the more you practice, the easier it becomes. I've seen this with the most successful people I know—it's all about repetition. If you embrace the concepts in Part 1 of this book with an open mind and then move on to the actionable steps in Part 2, I believe you will find success. Practice with the exercises in Part 2, and when it's time to make a big change, you'll be ready.

I'm not chasing any particular outcome with this venture—I'm not expecting to make millions. Breaking even is the goal. What matters most is that it's done, and it will be part of my legacy. At any point in the future, whether for my kids, my grandkids, or even my great-great-grandkids, this book will be a piece of me, preserved through time, as long as the technology still exists.

I did it, and that's what this book is here for—to show you that you can do it too.

Thank you for investing your time in reading this book I hope it serves you well, and I'd love to hear your feedback, good or bad. Remember, **Nothing Changes When Nothing Changes**.

Sincerely,

John 'J.D.' Ploetz

Contents

Foreword

I was seven when my parents divorced. After that, my mom had to pick up two extra jobs just to make ends meet. I learned a lot from her during that time—how to work hard, how to hustle, and how to pick yourself up when you're down.

It was also the first time I was exposed to the idea of getting caught in a cycle you can't escape. My mother worked insane hours to provide for my sister and me, but at the end of the day, she was right where she started. At the end of the month? Still in the same place.

I found myself in similar situations as I grew up—moving fast but staying in the same spot. I bartended, bussed tables, and even bought old Bowflex machines and resold them on Craigslist. Hustling was all I knew, so that's what I did.

Then I got into the garage door business, and things were going great... until they weren't. I made a series of bad decisions that compounded until I eventually found myself $50,000 in debt.

I can remember exactly where I was when I realized how deep in I was. I was sitting in my office at about 9 p.m. in June of 2008. I had no employees, and my business partner had jumped ship. All I had was a stack of unpaid bills about a mile high.

I remember thinking to myself at that moment, "I have to make this work."

I didn't just work hard to make that happen, though. I mean, I worked my ass off, but that's not how I broke out. I got my break by making small, incremental changes that eventually led to big, revolutionary changes. Now, A1 Garage Door Services is an empire worth over $220 million and counting.

But the best part of the position I'm in today is being able to hire and work with people like JD. Addiction, divorce, false accusations—

this is a guy who has been caught in some of the toughest cycles you can imagine. And he's come out on the other side as one of my favorite A1 success stories.

I've known JD for about a decade now. When he first came to me, he was a straight-up worker—super reliable, always open to feedback, and could fix a garage door like no other.

But he also had, and still has, the kind of heart that can be extremely rare in this business. When he's sitting in your house talking to you about a garage door, you know he's talking about things that will help you and your family the same way he would if it were his own family. He wasn't worrying about his sales bonus. In fact, he's the kind of guy who would lose that bonus just to watch you succeed.

I could always tell that JD wanted more, though. He wanted to grow, and he wanted to lead. And in order to get there, he was willing to change.

It has been extremely gratifying watching JD become the kind of leader he is today. And he never lost his heart in the process, either. He cares deeply about his employees—especially the ones he coaches and mentors. And because of his lessons, I've seen so many grow into the kind of A players we all need to build a lasting legacy.

JD has three grandchildren, and as of today, a fourth on the way. I know he couldn't be prouder. Ultimately, everything he's done has been so his family could live the life they've always dreamed of. Now, those dreams are all coming true. And after applying the lessons JD lays out in the pages ahead, I think yours will, too.

Tommy Mello
CEO, A1 Garage Doors

Part 1

Nothing Changes When Nothing Changes (NCWNC): Universal blueprint for Meaningful change & Long-term Success

Part 1: Introduction

Welcome to the first part of "Nothing Changes When Nothing Changes." This section delves into the personal side of this project—how and why it came to be. The title, Nothing Changes When Nothing Changes(NCWNC), encapsulates a concept that has been a cornerstone of my life both personally and professionally: when you don't make changes, nothing in your life will change. Initially, I assumed this concept was universally understood, but I realized over time that many people don't grasp its significance. This realization has driven me to help my coworkers and others understand that meaningful change is essential for advancement and success in various aspects of life. Through my experiences, I've seen how transformative this mindset can be.

Part 1 shares these experiences and the concepts that have guided me to greater success. You'll find personal anecdotes, lessons learned, and insights into how embracing change has positively impacted my life and the lives of those around me. Moving on to Part 2, you'll encounter a more structured step-by-step guide designed to help you advance toward success in multiple areas of your life. This section serves as a practical manual, offering detailed instructions and strategies. Extensive research ensures that Part 2 addresses as many aspects of personal and professional development as possible, aiming to answer a wide range of questions and provide actionable advice for those seeking to improve their lives.

As you read through Part 1, you'll get to know the personal journey behind the principles laid out in this book. I will give you the NCWNC WHO, WHAT, WHEN, WHERE and most importantly the WHY: Why this book was written.

1

Chapter 1: WHO

I'm thrilled you've picked up this book, thank you! If you're anything like me, you're in the trenches, hustling and navigating life's twists and turns every day. I'm here to share what I've learned from my journey, hoping it will illuminate yours.

With positive thinking and a commitment to change, I've made great strides in my personal and professional life. I'm still a work in progress, but the progress has been significant. That's why I wrote this book—to share what I know and to help you on your journey.

I've been fortunate to witness and appreciate the changes and progress in myself and my colleagues, often on a daily basis. I know what I'm talking about and writing about works because I see its impact every day in my life and in the lives of those with whom I work.

I have been through "stuff" in my life and made it to the other side. You will soon learn in detail some of that "stuff."

Why am I telling you this? Because I want you to know that I've probably been exactly where you are. Whether you are on cloud nine or in a difficult place, I've been there, and that is not a bad thing. Life is life. Just like you I've had some very high highs and some very low lows. I think most people have. I've felt stuck, frustrated, and unsure of what to do next. That's why I believe what I have to say can actually help you. No matter the scenario you are in. I'm not coming from some lofty, unattainable place. I'm coming from experience—the kind you can relate to, the kind that's real, unabashed, and honest. The real deal.

There are a lot of self-help books out there, and all of them are good in their own right for one reason or another, I'm sure. I haven't read all of them, of course, but I have been through quite a few. There was a time in my life that I grasped for just about anything to get out of where I was at, and I used a lot of what I read. The problem I ran into was I had to go to many different sources to get what I needed, or thought I needed at the time. So when putting this together, I decided to have as much information as I could possibly get in one place, so when you read this can have the information you need in one place.

Most self-help books are written by well-known individuals—celebrities, academics, or public figures with some degree of fame. Readers often pick up these books hoping to emulate their success, which is a positive aspiration. Like those esteemed authors, my goal is to help you achieve and even surpass your ambitions.

Now, I might not be famous, but trust me when I say I'm in a pretty good place. And yes, I know that's a tall order, but stick with me—I'll convince you soon enough. You could do a lot worse than emulate me! When I say I'm in a good place, I mean it. Whenever someone asks how I'm doing, I tell them, "I'm good, life is uneventful, and any problems I have are just mere inconveniences." Spoiler alert: it hasn't always been that way, as you'll soon find out.

I have goals and dreams just like you. Right now, I'm dreaming of retiring in the next decade (or sooner if I can swing it). We all have dreams and goals, and this book is a fantastic first step. It will get you moving in a positive direction, 100%.

The purpose of this book is to show you that there's more to life if you want it, and achieving success isn't some big secret or mystery.

It's totally achievable with the right mindset and a bit of elbow grease. This book is your all-around guide to getting on the right track or a better track. No matter what part of your life you want to change or improve, the information here will help you do just that!

I believe, no, I know, success comes from understanding, being open-minded, embracing change, working hard, and sometimes following in the footsteps of those who have faced similar challenges. Overcoming obstacles and navigating through life's difficulties with the least resistance are also as important. When you wrap them all together you have the perfect storm (in a good way) to catapult out of a static, stagnant life into successes you never thought possible. What is here will help you navigate to the eye of that perfect storm and use it to your advantage everyday of your life, if you so choose. The principles in this book are so powerful to some, entire lives and generations have and will be changed because of them.

As I write this book, I'm 57 years old, soon to be 58. Currently, I'm an Area Manager for A1 Garage Door Service, overseeing 30+ technicians, across 2 major markets. In this position I am responsible for about $20 million in annual revenue. My journey in the garage door business began as a technician, and over the last decade, I've worked my way up to my current position.

I'm also a proud father of five grown children—two boys and two girls with my X wife and a stepson from my current relationship. I love them all very much. Being a father has been the most challenging and most rewarding area of my adult life. I am blessed to also have three grandchildren and another on the way. I've been divorced for over ten years, following an 18-year up and down marriage. You also need to know I am a very proud dog father of three fantastic K9's. Two Pugs, Miss Zoe and Miss Ruby and a Poodle mix, Miss Kitty. All spoiled beyond normal circumstances! Today, I own a house, a car, have very little debt, and boast (not brag) a FICO score over 800—a significant improvement from the 300s where it languished for most of my life. This turnaround is a testament to the changes I made and the principles I now share in this book, which also led to financial stability. Notice I said stability and not independence. Still working on that. Perhaps that will be the topic of my next book!

I have a wonderful life partner, Lisa, whom I wouldn't trade for the world. I'm pretty sure she would trade me off in a heartbeat if the right deal came along !! Even with our differences we are a great team and we are committed to being together forever, whatever that may look like.

For recreation we love exploring the outdoors in our side by side, camp and love working on our 1953 home. It is in a constant state of re-model. Between the two of us we have a lot of hobbies. Christmas is a very festive time in our house and that is the time our creativeness really shines, or glows, as it were!

From the above paragraphs you can decipher a number of challenges I have faced and had to overcome. All pretty normal life stuff—debt, work pressures, divorce, and the demands of raising children as a single parent. While I don't view my kids as obstacles, any parent knows they come with their own set of challenges. Just like you, I've navigated these obstacles and came out stronger. This is part of my case to get you to trust me.

With 58 years of life experience, I've realized that everyone successful in any area of life shares one common trait. It's something you can't bypass, cheat, fake or buy. That trait is the genuine willingness to do it. Willingness is one of the toughest mindsets for most people to adopt and practice.

Willingness! Do you have the willingness to change to be successful? Ask yourself honestly right now! Do you want to change whatever comforts and obstacles are holding you back? Are you willing to do that? Can you apply the necessary, sometimes painful, changes that need to happen to stop the static life you're in? I hope so. I did, and I'm still doing it. Some changes were easier for me to embrace than others. It's the tougher changes—the ones that really challenge you—that will truly move the needle toward success. These are the changes that require the most practice, persistence, and of course, willingness.

The good news is that willingness to make changes isn't an all-or-nothing deal. As with all the guidance in this book, willingness can come in small parts, but it must come in some form. If not, you're just fooling yourself. Wanting change without being willing to do what it takes is called wishful thinking. Wishful thinking will kill success even before it starts.

I have a whole section on this later, but let's focus on willingness for now and how to get started with it.

Think of willingness as a muscle that grows stronger with each small effort. Just as lifting light weights over time builds strength, applying small, consistent changes in your life gradually transforms your static situation. It's not about making one grand, painful change overnight; it's about taking manageable steps that lead to significant progress. The good news is each small act of willingness adds up, just like each rep at the gym builds muscle. Start small and watch your life transform one step at a time. As you conquer a few small steps with willingness, apply that to the change you want to make, and before you know it, you are growing in ways you never thought possible. Having that willingness, no matter how small, will give you the ability to change. Nothing Changes When Nothing Changes!

So, you have the willingness, right? You've decided to make a change! Embracing change is the next crucial step. Change is all-encompassing, life-altering, and necessary. Your life is going to change, I guarantee that, with or without your approval. While some changes are beyond our control, positive change is one aspect where you have full control. You have the power to make positive changes—100%. 24/7/365. There are no days when change can't happen! The day and time you want it to start is up to you. I'm using the word change a lot, why? Because it is important to understand. Have you ever really thought about what change means?

Webster's defines change in its verb form as:
  – To make different in some particular: alter

  – To make radically different: transform

  – To give a different position, course, or direction to

Change is a verb, an action word. If you desire change, you need to take action. No way around it. Your potential is unlocked by your actions and your actions only.

Besides witnessing changes in my life and others around me, I have had a front-row seat to change and transformation at my workplace. One of the people I've been fortunate enough to watch and learn from is the owner of A1 Garage Door Service. He is a big-picture thinker, a visionary, and a genuinely nice, down-to-earth man. I say with out hesitation 'One of a kind'.

I've been lucky to observe and be part of the growth and transformation of the company and, in turn, his transformation to what they are today. Tommy Mello started this company years ago with the help of his mother and stepfather. Through dedication and hard work, he has turned a one-van home service company into a multi-million dollar operation! This success came from his willingness to embrace change. He didn't get to where he is today by doing the same thing every day. He surrounded himself with people who also embraced change, leading to exponential growth. We are still growing!

One of Tommy's favorite phrases is, "Today, I'm the best I've ever been but the worst I'll ever be, because tomorrow I'll be a little bit better". This phrase perfectly encapsulates the essence of change and serves as an excellent motto for individuals and businesses alike. As a business, we are in uncharted territory in the home service industry, especially in the garage door sector. We embraced change, welcomed it, and with the willingness to do what it takes, we get the job done every day.

I love being part of the A1 family. Without the opportunity Tommy gave me many years ago, I wouldn't be where I am today—in this position in life, this career, and with the opportunities yet to come. Tommy is an inspiration to thousands of people. He is energetic and transparent in the way he conducts his life and the way he runs his business. He truly cares about each employee at A1 and genuinely wants them to succeed in life. He bends over backwards for his team and makes sure everyone has what they need to succeed if they choose to do so. That is why I asked him to write the foreword to this book. I could go on for hours about Tommy and all that he has done for me and hundreds of others. Just Google him if you want to know more. Well worth the time!

In a way, he is the reason for this undertaking. Without his example and my front-row seat to see exactly what change can accomplish, I'd never have attempted this book. Thank you, Tommy

Now that you know where I'm at today and have a brief explanation of how I got here, I want to do something that most authors wouldn't do. I'm going to further convince you that what I'm talking about actually works by sharing some of the more challenging places I've been and emerged from stronger. Remember the steps I took to move past these experiences are the same steps for you and anyone else trying to get to the other side of a situation.

Recognize that change is needed.

Develop the willingness to change.

Take the necessary steps to implement that change. I know that sounds simplistic, but we will cover all of this in great detail coming up.

You might be thinking this list can't be that bad and say, "My situation is way worse!" Maybe, but to most of you I say, " Stop right there and hold my beer!" (figuratively of course). Let me share a bit of my sordid past—not to compare hardships but to show you that even from the darkest places, change and success are possible when you realize Nothing Changes When nothing Changes.

Ready!!!

I have a total of eight DUIs, yes, I said eight! They were across three states and over a span of 25 years. My last one was well over a decade ago, and it finally brought me to the point of seeking recovery. Today, I am sober. You can imagine the turmoil and hurdles that come with each DUI and the effort required to regain a semblance of a normal life. It takes years to put just a single DUI behind you. Time, money, jobs, and friends—all lost every time.

I remember my first DUI in Arizona when I was about 20. I spent 24 hours in jail, attended mandatory classes, and paid a fine of around $450. My last DUI was far more severe: three months in jail, classes, counseling, and meetings for over a year, and a staggering cost of $25,000. That 25k was just for fines and fees associated with the DUI. It does not include Attorneys fees and other related costs. It was a lot to come back from.

Going further, I've faced some incredibly difficult situations, including being falsely accused of crimes I didn't commit. The worst of these was being accused of rape in the Bahamas. If the accuser hadn't eventually told the truth, I might still be in a Bahamian jail, where I spent two harrowing weeks. I wasn't even in the vicinity of the alleged crime at the time; the accuser fabricated the entire story because she didn't want to get in trouble with her parents for coming in late again. When asked why she chose me, she said my name was the easiest to remember and the first one she could think of. It was a pretty raw deal.

The accusation was eventually proven false beyond a shadow of a doubt, and I was cleared of any involvement. However, the damage had been done. Being processed and incarcerated in The Bahamas during the early 90's was like being in a show of Barney Miller. The entire process was all hand done. NO COMPUTERS! Reports by hand, statements by hand, it took forever. As you might imagine the accommodations were not very good either. You have all seen cells in old westerns, right? Well, that's it. I'm not kidding!

In the end just the accusation left me without a job and forced me to start over once I returned to the States. Getting back to the States, specifically to Arizona, was an ordeal in itself. When I was finally released I was put outside the gate of the village where I had been working and told to leave. I had no money, no friends, and was completely alone. I had to get very creative to find my way back to the States. That trip back would be a great topic of another book! It was that crazy!

Despite these dark times, I can tell you with great certainty that the person I am today is not even close to the one who was in the middle of those situations. These experiences taught me resilience and the importance of perseverance. Again, proving over and over that change is possible. Using the same processes and thoughts in this book, I emerged stronger and more determined. Why share all of this? I want you to know that change is possible, even from the darkest places in life.

Those were some of the more extreme examples, and I understand that not everyone will relate to them. If thinking about these situations feels surreal to you, let's shift to other, less extreme instances that are still true. These might be more relateable for those who couldn't connect with the earlier examples.

As I mentioned before, I've been through a divorce after 18 years of marriage. It's never an easy place to come back from, emotionally or financially. This divorce also happened with four kids, adding to the complexity and difficulty. Divorce is common in this country, and it is sad. My ex and I tried for years to make it work. I know for a fact that some of you can relate to the challenges in that situation.

Over the years, I've lost several jobs. Anyone who's been through that knows how destructive and life-changing it can be. Most of them I can attribute to my addiction—usually drinking. I drank my way out of a couple of jobs that would have been life-changing in many ways, had I been able to keep them. However, for clarity, I'm not blaming my addiction for any loses in my life. All of the past is my doing and mine alone I take full responsibility for my actions, past, present, and future. Losing a job under any circumstances is difficult. Every time it happened I had to start over and begin the process of positive, constructive change, and I did.

I hope you understand that you don't need to experience a disaster or a significant downturn in life to seek improvement, change, or success. I gave these examples because, like I have done in the past, I believe some people pick up a book like this to find ways to overcome immediate challenges they face. They need answers or a plan. I just wanted to reassure those readers that it will be OK, and they made a good choice by seeking guidance here. You don't have to be in a bad place to benefit from this book, and I hope you're not. The key point is that no matter where you are on the happiness spectrum, a willingness to change is essential to transform any situation. Remember, Nothing Changes When Nothing Changes.

Those are just a few examples of places I have been, always coming out stronger. If I can do it, you guessed it, you can do it. I just want to let you know I'm a person who's been through some bad stuff, made it to the other side, and used the things I talk about in this book to get there. Of course, 20+ years ago I wasn't aware of some of these techniques, but looking back I can see how I was using them even without knowing it. I do remember people reaching out to help me, and some of the techniques they talked about are right here. Most have been around for a long time. The problem is people hear things differently at different ages and at different points in their life. Sometimes you are not in a place to accept them at the time. I know I was not back then, but they always stuck with me. When I was ready to use them, I had them in my toolbox.

My hope for you is, it will make it that much easier for you to take that next step in life. Whether you're just static and need to move forward, or you're going through some serious shit and need to get to the other side. Success is within reach; I promise you that! By putting together the philosophies and thought processes, along with the actionable items in Part 2, You can overcome anything! The only thing stopping you, is you! You're going to hear that a lot here because you're the only person who can change your situation. Here are a few of my favorite clichés for this.

"You are your own greatest obstacle and your own greatest ally."

"Change begins with you."

"The only thing standing between you and your goals is you."

I'm very fond of clichés. The reason, is because they are easy to remember and at 58 I need easy. Seriously, if you really think about them, they can help. Actually, I know they can! One more, "You are the master of your own destiny." How very true that is! You now know the WHO. Now on to the WHAT!

2

Chapter 2: WHAT

WHAT is this book about? In its simplest form, this book is about sparking a change—a change in your life. What happens after that change could be a million different things. How big will the change be? Who knows? Remember, it doesn't have to be some monumental shift to move things in a forward direction.

There are millions, if not billions, of people on this Earth who want something more out of life than what they currently have. Most of those people will never move past where they are, and the reason for that is simple: they are unwilling to make a change. I dive into this in more detail in the 'WHY' chapter, but for now, let's focus on the WHAT.

This book is about giving you the inspiration and tools to invoke a change in your life to move forward in any area you desire—whether it's financial, personal, business, recreational, or whatever. It's all possible. But here's the kicker: you're the only person who can do this. No one else can do it for you. Sound familiar?

This book is about equipping you with the knowledge and tools to transform any facet of your life into something different, hopefully that will lead to a desired outcome. Human beings are incredibly resilient and capable of so much. Yet, very few of us do what needs to be done to advance our lives and become a little more successful, a little happier, a little wealthier. We settle for the status quo and stop dreaming, stop wanting more and start believing that it's a huge leap to move beyond just getting by. This is not true. It just takes a little— a little time, a little learning, a little desire. That's the key: a little. A little at a time. Not huge shifts. Huge can work, but huge is rarely followed through on or finished. If you're like me, I had problems finishing things I started. That must change. Finishing what you start from here on out is very important. Even when the outcome is not what you desired or what you were shooting for. Finishing is the key. It will take practice and perseverance. I did it. You most certainly can.

When it comes to personal growth, it's not just about setting objectives but about achieving them and not saying "I QUIT'. It's about reaching each milestone, meeting your targets, and following through with your plans. The key isn't just in what you aspire to do but in accomplishing the tasks you set for yourself. By focusing on completion points and seeing each step through, you'll find real progress and transformation. Instead of merely setting goals, think in terms of finish lines, completion points, and action steps. This way, you emphasize the importance of the process and the act of completing tasks, ensuring that each step you take leads to tangible results and personal growth.

The opposite of all this is quitting. Quitting will never get you anywhere, no matter how much you try to convince yourself otherwise. Quitting is TOXIC to any success you might want to achieve. Quitting is F'ed up—I can't put it any more plainly. Failure is not the same as quitting. Failure is simply reaching the end without achieving the desired or most positive outcome.

Quitting means giving up before you've given yourself a chance to succeed. It's a surrender to obstacles rather than a challenge to overcome them. Failure, on the other hand, is a part of the journey.

It's a lesson, a stepping stone, and an opportunity to grow stronger and wiser. You will fail and that is part of Success. The point is you finished and failed, which is good.

When you fail, you gain insights into what didn't work, and that knowledge is invaluable. It's through failure that you learn, adapt, and eventually find the path to success. Quitting deprives you of that chance to learn and improve.

Remember, every successful person has faced failure. The difference is they didn't quit; they kept pushing forward. Embrace failure as a necessary part of your journey, but never let it lead to quitting. The power to change and achieve your goals lies within you, and the only thing standing in your way is the decision to keep going, no matter what.

Quitting, bad. Failure, good. Got it? Good.

Completing a goal or task takes steps. Actionable, achievable steps. You don't jump from minimum wage to multi-millionaire in a single leap. A lot of the time, it takes just a little patience! Unfortunately, the human condition doesn't exactly favor patience. So, hopefully, you'll understand that change is a process, not a magic wand.

Good old patience—a dirty word to most. Patience is a tricky thing, often very challenging. It is a skill that must be learned by most. People who have a handle on it generally outshine those who do not. Just my opinion. Patience is a great tool and should be embraced, practiced and viewed as an asset. Unfortunately, people often think of it in a negative light. After years of practice, I still struggle with it, but I see it as a great friend when I can muster it. A friend that has helped me out of some very difficult situations. We all need patience with the DMV (when they had them), children, other drivers, co-workers, Costco.....Just to name a few. When you have patience, the entire world looks different......and the world looks at you differently.

Dare I? Ok, I will. Remember *"Patience is a virtue."*

Through my observation and self-reflection, I believe people are inherently impatient, often preferring immediate rewards over larger rewards that require waiting. Most of you likely already recognize this. What you may not know is that this tendency is deeply rooted in our psychological makeup. Even short delays can cause significant impatience, emphasizing how much we value immediacy and quick results in our decision-making processes. It almost seems we are wired to be impatient. We all need to have more patience. If we can, the path to success and change will be that much faster and error free.

Good things come to those who wait!

Impatience can also be linked to the modern world's fast-paced, technology-driven environment, where instant gratification is the norm. People today often expect things to happen quickly and can become frustrated when faced with delays, whether in traffic, waiting for a package, or even during election results.

Moreover, our brains are wired to find waiting unpleasant. The discomfort of waiting tends to increase as the wait progresses, driven by our desire for closure and resolution. This need for closure can lead us to make hasty decisions just to alleviate the feeling of uncertainty and impatience. If you are like me and generally impatient, please be aware of that, then plan and act on it accordingly. Personally, I do a lot of deep breathing and counting when I get in a situation when I'm feeling inpatient. It works for me most of the time. You will have to navigate it in your own way, but navigate it you will have to do!

So, it's important to understand that achieving meaningful change is a process, not a quick fix. Embracing patience and understanding that worthwhile changes take time can help manage expectations and improve outcomes in the long run.

Haste makes waste!

So closing out this chapter, the NCWNC 'WHAT' is change! Remember, change is a journey, not a destination. This book is here to help you start that journey, giving you the tools and knowledge to transform any part of your life. Whether it's financial, personal, business, or just for fun, the potential for change is right there inside you. All it takes is a little time, a little learning, and a little desire.

Think about the challenges I've shared—from divorce to losing jobs. Even in those tough times, I managed to turn things around, and so can you. It's all about setting goals, completing tasks, and pushing through failures. Quitting is never an option; failure is just a lesson on your way to success. Patience might be tough, but it's your friend. Remember, meaningful change takes time, and every small step counts.

So, take a deep breath, stay patient, and keep moving forward. You've got this! The power to change is within you, and with each small step you're getting closer to your desired outcome. Remember, nothing changes when nothing changes. The WHEN is next!

3

Chapter 3: WHEN

When? When do you need this book? When should you use this book? The answer is NOW. "There's no time like the present!" That seems simple enough, right? Well, not so much. There are plenty of other people, places, and things out there in your world that want your NOW (your immediate attention) more than you do. They'll fight tooth and nail for it, and a lot of folks will hand their NOW over without a second thought. You've got to be a little selfish with your NOW. (your time). You're worth the change you're trying to implement. Once you're through this book from cover to cover, you'll need to carve out time to put those plans into action. If you don't, excuses will creep in, and that change you so desire and need, will end up gathering dust on the metaphorical treadmill with all the other things you never got around to using. Procrastination will creep in.

So, grab your NOW, hold it tight, and let's get started on making that change happen!

We talked about patience in the last chapter. Along with patience not always being our friend when it comes to change, we also have another P word! Procrastination. I call these the two killer P's. One you have to learn to use and the other you need to eliminate completely.

Patience and Procrastination. Some of my favorite clichés have these 2 words in them. All so true.

"Patience is a virtue, but procrastination is the thief of time."

"Patience brings rewards, procrastination brings regrets."

"Patience leads to progress, procrastination leads to panic."

"With patience, success is possible; with procrastination, it's impossible."

Procrastination is a long, ugly, hard to spell word! Bottom line, procrastination must be managed to make any meaningful change in your life. Some people make jokes about procrastination. That's fine, but when you really think about how much time you waste because of it, it really isn't funny at all. Maybe you aren't a procrastinator. That is great. I struggled with it for years and still do from time to time. Personally, I've made significant progress in overcoming procrastination. Like any other change I've had to make, it took consistent steps to achieve positive results. It definitely didn't happen overnight—far from it!

PRO-CRAST-I-NA-TION....Ugggg . I know for me, I can be an expert at procrastinating. I can tell myself any number of reasons why I don't need to do something right now. The excuses are endless, and I think for a lot of people it is the exact same thing. That is why you're going to hear a lot about accountability later in the book. Accountability is a Procrastination Assassin! We won't dive into accountability right now—there's plenty more on that in a much better place in the book— just know that procrastination is real, can be crippling and it affects most everyone, directly or indirectly. The indirect damage Procrastination has is unbelievable. Just one act from one person can have a ripple effect on dozens of other people.

Procrastination can have severe negative impacts on our lives. It's not just about putting things off until the last minute; it's a habit that can significantly affect our health, relationships, and overall well-being. Chronic procrastinators often face increased stress and anxiety, which can lead to health issues such as high blood pressure and cardiovascular diseases.

Procrastinators are also more likely to delay necessary medical and dental check-ups, further jeopardizing their health. Furthermore, procrastination can result in a significant loss of time. You only have one life, and every time you put off your dreams and goals, you waste precious time you will never get back. This can lead to a deep sense of regret and frustration later in life when you realize how much more you could have achieved if you had only taken that first step earlier.

In terms of relationships, procrastination can cause frustration and disappointment among loved ones. They may feel neglected or unimportant when plans are canceled or promises are not kept due to procrastination. This can lead to a cycle of distrust and resentment, severely damaging relationships over time.

Additionally, procrastination is often tied to how we manage our emotions rather than just our time. Chronic procrastinators tend to prioritize immediate mood repair over long-term goals, leading to a cycle of stress and avoidance.

Recognizing the detrimental effects of procrastination can be the first step toward making meaningful changes and improving various aspects of life. Taking proactive steps can lead to better health, stronger relationships, and a more fulfilling life.

It's important to understand that procrastination is a real issue that affects most everyone. It's something that needs to be addressed head-on. Just like with patience, recognizing the problem is the first step toward overcoming it. This book will provide you with the tools and strategies to tackle procrastination, ensuring that you can move forward and achieve your goals.

The "WHEN" for this book, is NOW! I know that seems simplistic because you're reading it now, but let's be real: as we have seen, human nature loves procrastination and dislikes patience (even though we shouldn't).We find all sorts of nutty reasons to not follow through with things, especially when it involves some sort of change. We don't like change, but to move forward from where we are right now, we must change something. Here are some more of my favorite clichés. These are for moving past procrastination. If you think about them, they all make sense. Use them when you are right in the middle of convincing yourself NOT to do something:

"The future starts now."

"Don't wait for the perfect moment, take the moment and make it perfect."

"Today is the first day of the rest of your life."

Have I convinced you yet? Now is the time to start the changes. Nothing Changes When Nothing Changes.

Taking the WHEN a step further when should you start using what you learn from reading or listening to this book? The honest answer... whenever you decide to. But let me tell you from experience—the sooner the better.

The information and insights in this book are here to help you make a change, and the quicker you act on them, the sooner you'll see results.

Believe me, I get it; change is difficult. It's uncomfortable. But if you keep waiting for the perfect moment to change something, you'll be waiting forever. As the saying goes, you can lead a horse to water, but you can't make it drink. This book can guide you, provide you with the tools and inspiration, but you're the one who must take the steps. So, don't wait. Don't procrastinate, dive in, take the concepts and steps to heart, keep an open mind, and start making those changes now. Your future self will thank you.

4

Chapter 4: WHERE

Before we dive into this chapter, I have a little secret to share with you about the origin of this book. It has been brewing in my mind for two or three years, and it became a serious project about a year ago. Not many people know I had been contemplating it for that long. Interestingly, the idea all started with Part 2. Initially, it was meant to be a resource for my techs to help them achieve more success in their lives.

I did extensive research, scouring the internet for actionable, achievable items my techs could use. Lisa and I would spend evenings making lists of things that could help them improve, not just at work but in life in general. Before long, we had compiled quite a list.

With that list in hand, I wanted to create something convincing, to show that change is possible through my example and the examples of others. That's when Part 1 began to take shape. So, the first inspiration for this book came from my spare time efforts to help my employees. I guess its not a secret anymore.

Simply put NCWNC came out of a need to help my Techs improve and strive for more. From the realization that change can be difficult, but absolutely achievable, I just had to convince them of that. Now, I'm trying to convince you of that!

I want to take a moment to discuss the importance of knowing your personal WHERE. This is the place you, as an individual, aspire to reach. Many of you reading this book may feel there's supposed to be more to your life—a nagging sense that something greater awaits you. I've felt that way my whole life. It's as if you're meant to do more and be more, but you just don't know how to get there. It's a voice in the back of your mind telling you that you can achieve more, that you can become so much more than you are today.

To get there, you need to know WHERE you're trying to go— your goal, the change, the outcome you desire. It's not always easy to identify. That little voice and feeling never go away. But I'm here to tell you that if you don't know all of that right now, it's okay. Just read, absorb, and you'll recognize it when it comes to you. Allow yourself the freedom to not know exactly where you're going; keep an open mind. Let the voice keep reminding you that there is more for you. Keep moving forward. Keep advancing somehow, never stagnate. I talk about being just 1% better every day to my employees, how making small improvements every day really adds up over time. If you keep taking little steps forward, you build a routine and get better at improving. Each step becomes easier because you know the process well. And then, when you eventually face a big challenge or need to make a significant change, it won't feel as overwhelming. You will be ready because you've kept moving forward and haven't let things get stagnant. Continuous little wins make the big wins more achievable. Keep doing that and when the WHERE gets clearer, you will be prepared! Shortly, I will talk about how to recognize and seize opportunities. Your WHERE is out there in the form of an opportunity that hasn't shown itself yet. Patience!

We aren't done with the WHERE yet.

I don't know about you, but I do some of my best thinking when I'm driving, especially on long trips. One day I was coming back from a scouting expedition in New Mexico. I was looking for camping spots for our 4th of July weekend trip. I spent a lot of time thinking about this particular chapter "WHERE". I started thinking about the word and what it meant in my life and the successful changes I have made. I came up with two conclusions that are below. This was a tough one to convey! I just wanted to let you know that this was not an easy one. Well, actually, none of it has been easy, but on the difficulty level, this chapter was at the top. So, here is what I came up with, and it really rang true the further I went and the more I wrote. I hope it rings loud and clear with you too. For the record I was not driving and writing. I was driving and dictating. I was being safe.

WHERE do you use the information in this book? I think for most of you it will come to you in one or maybe both of the following scenarios. First, there's the philosophical "WHERE" and second, the literal "WHERE."

Philosophical WHERE.

Alright, let's get into the philosophical side of "WHERE." Think of "where" as your current state of mind and heart rather than your physical location. It's about being mentally and emotionally ready to make changes and get the most out of this book. Whether you're at the peak of your career or dealing with personal struggles, it doesn't matter. It's keeping an open mind. I guess the easiest way to explain it is you're in a place WHERE you can allow yourself to move forward and make changes. Remember, we are the only one that is going to stop us from making the changes we desire to get to the Where we want to be. So keep this WHERE wide open for anything!

Physical WHERE

Second is the physical WHERE. Your surroundings play a significant role in your ability to achieve the goals and changes you want. Here are some ideas to help keep your physical WHERE conducive to making the necessary changes. The more you can do to keep your current WHERE clutter-free, the better off you will be—literally and figuratively.

Create a productive environment: stay organized and find quiet areas for reflection and planning. A clutter-free, well-organized space can do wonders for your mindset and motivation.

Next, consider your job. Is your work environment supportive? Does it help you grow? Sometimes changing your physical workspace or even finding a new job can unlock new opportunities and foster personal growth.

Now, let's talk about health. Your physical and mental health are crucial. Making changes to your health routine can have a profound impact on your overall well-being and ability to make other changes in your life. Feeling good is huge factor in success.

Lastly, don't forget your support systems. Surround yourself with supportive people—family, friends, mentors, or professional networks. These relationships create an environment where change is not only possible but encouraged. Creating the right environment for your current state is crucial. Start by organizing your personal space. Surround yourself with positive influences. Look for and act on opportunities for growth in all areas of your life.

Remember, the "WHERE" is not just a physical location. It's a mental and emotional state, a supportive community, and the opportunities you create and seize. This chapter is dedicated to helping you start to find your "WHERE." To get you to start thinking about WHERE this information is going to help you. Hopefully, something will click, and you'll realize that's the area of your life that needs change. I know for a fact, some of you are reading this and have no idea WHERE to start. Maybe you're even more confused than when you stared reading. Don't sweat it. There are going to be light bulb or "ah-ha" moments throughout this book. Many of them, I hope, in the next chapter, "Why."

It was as if a switch had been flipped and the darkness was replaced by brilliant clarity.

5

Chapter 5: WHY (The light bulb chapter)

As I've said before, this book has been rolling around in my head for years, and now it's finally coming to fruition. It's been quite a journey! So far in Nothing Changes When Nothing Changes we've covered the "who," "what," "when," and "where." Now we're at the "why." This is the heart of PART 1—Saved for last, the coup de gras, the holy NCWNC grail! ....The reason and thought process behind the changes, how I made changes, how I help others make changes, and how I've seen people make changes and be successful. Everything you need to mix together to make this "Success" recipe work!

It's no secret that certain ideas and concepts are crucial for change to happen. There are thousands of self-help books, each with its own purpose and specificity. Despite their differences, they share common themes that must be embraced for them to be effective. That's what this chapter is about. Feel free to read it multiple times if needed. It's crucial for you to understand these ideas.

Don't freak out! It's not some complicated formula, and please do not overthink them. Take them at face value and don't read anything into them. The bottom line is: unless you can embrace, agree with, or at least recognize the truth in the concepts we're about to discuss, nothing else matters. Its nothing crazy, nothing controversial; it's common sense, as you will see. These concepts are essential for allowing the changes you want to happen.

So, let's dive in. If you're skeptical, I encourage you to adopt a "fake it till you make it" mindset and read on. Even if you think I'm full of BS, you won't be able to un-read these ideas and will have gotten my points across. Once you start to experience the changes, your buy-in will become more solidified—I guarantee it. Trust the process, allow the change to happen, and you'll see the difference for yourself.

So, what is change? What is success? And WHY did I write this book? Most importantly, WHY will it work for you? First, a few definitions, so we are all on the same page. We talked about change earlier and its definition. I need to expand on that a bit.

Change:

Change is the act of making something different from what it was before. It involves transforming or modifying aspects of a situation, behavior, or condition. Change can happen in many areas of life, driven by various factors, and often marks a transition from one state to another. That's the literal definition of change and it works for our purposes. The big takeaway: change is modifying or transforming something.

Next definition.

Success:

Success can mean different things to different people, depending on where you're at in life, what you want to accomplish, and where you've been. Success is achieving a desired goal or outcome, whether in personal, professional, or other areas of life. It's often marked by the fulfillment of ambitions and the attainment of meaningful results. Success is measured in small and large increments, both of which are impactful, depending on your perspective. I measure/monitor my success by my attitude. If my attitude is positive and worth sharing, I have been successful in whatever my endeavor was. When I wake up and go about my day with a feeling of contentment, and purpose I'm successful. Everyone will measure success differently, but you will know it when you have it.

Success doesn't always mean a big house, an expensive car, and lots of cash. For some, waking up and walking just a few miles is a huge success. Then others might dream of being able to do just that and when they do accomplish just ONE mile it is a HUGE success. Success is relative to one's current state and thoughts. What is a great success to you might just be another ho-hum day to someone else and visa versa. Never play folly to another persons thought of success. Celebrate and encourage people's successes whenever you can. Remember, small wins are important, and many people can't even achieve what you might take for granted as successful. Change and Success go hand in hand. You cannot have one without the other.

'You can't be successful at change unless you change something successfully!"

WHY did I write this book?

I've touched on this a few times in the previous chapters, but here's the pointed answer: I wrote this book because I've experienced significant changes in my own life that have led to success in many areas. I've been fortunate enough to apply what I've learned to help others personally and professionally. In turn I have watched them become more successful too. As the old saying goes, I want to share the wealth.

The realization that the methods and principles I use could genuinely help others motivated me to share them more broadly, beyond just my technicians and friends.

Much of what I know, and practice, comes from my experiences and the lessons I've learned from my employer. Not all, of course, but Tommy and A1 gave me the freedom to push the envelope and experiment until I got it mostly right. It will never be 100% perfect, and I'm okay with that. I operate on the 80/20 rule: if a process is followed, it will work effectively 80% of the time. The remaining 20% accounts for one-offs, odd situations, and other factors that can disrupt the process. So, I focus on the 80% that works and let go and learn from the 20% that doesn't, ensuring that the core process for the change remains strong and reliable. In summary, the reason I wrote this book is to share the strategies and actions that have worked for me and others. It's not rocket science or a secret formula; it's a collection of well-thought-out ideas coupled with actionable steps that can lead to real change and success. I wanted to give everyone the chance to benefit from what I've discovered and applied in my own life and work.

WHY will it work for you?

I can't guarantee it will work for you specifically, but I believe it will, and here's why. The concepts in this book are simple and straightforward. They aren't far-fetched or mysterious; they are common-sense principles that, when combined, can ignite change. The second reason is the actionable items provided in Part Two. These are clear, step-by-step instructions for applying the principles to various areas of your life. There's no guesswork involved. If you embrace the principles in Part One and follow the steps that apply to your situation or desired change in Part Two, I believe anyone can be successful in any endeavor. I've tried to encompass as many forms of successful actions in Part Two as possible. Whether it's improving your finances, relationships, time management, or any number of different actionable items, the goal is to drive you out of a static life.

Some portions of this book you might use immediately, some you might use a year from now, and some you may never use. But I've put together a vast amount of information that covers a broad spectrum for anyone looking to break out of their stagnant life and make a change.

Without exception, most self-help books present a philosophy, or a series of steps designed to guide you through whatever challenges you face. This book is no different. We're talking about change, meaningful, impactful Change. That's a big deal. For all big deals to work you need a plan....Here is that plan!

The very first step in any meaningful change is recognizing that change is needed. You've already taken that step without even knowing it. The fact that you're reading this indicates that you're aware something in your life needs to change. Simple, right? That's number one and clearly the most obvious step toward change.

For instance when you say, "I need to change something," "I want more money in my bank account, how can I do that?", "There must be a better way to work out, what are my options?" or "I'm not happy with my current station in life, what can I do?" you're sparking the initial step toward change. That step, In a word: awareness. This awareness is the spark that ignites the journey of change. As soon as you think about changing something, as soon as you say you want to change something you have started the wheels in motion. You have started a process that can change your life. What are you going do with it is the question!

Once you have made the decision knowing change is needed you next need to understand two key aphorisms: "Nothing changes when nothing changes" and "You only know what you know." These phrases aren't just philosophies; they are aphorisms—concise, memorable expressions of general truths or principles. That was fancy way of saying they are common sense. They are so obvious that you really can't argue with them Truth of Truths! To me, they perfectly encapsulate principles that are undeniable and easy to remember. Honestly, when we break most self-help books down to their most basic form, including this one, they hinge on that first simple truth: Nothing Changes When Nothing Changes. If you don't make any changes, your current situation, attitude, or overall life circumstances, everything will remain the same. I have come to love those 5 words and that's why it's the title of this book!

When you truly grasp the concept of "Nothing Changes When Nothing Changes," you must also recognize that making any change requires action. Remember, action is key. This action involves expanding your knowledge. Knowledge can mean broadening your understanding, perception, or insight on any subject you want to improve.

To act differently, think differently, and ultimately be different, you need more information. Your current thinking and knowledge have brought you to where you are now, and if that's not where you want to be, it's time for a change. You want to move past your current situation, which is why you're seeking change.

You only know what you know, right? Now, it's time to take action and expand that knowledge.

Here's your first ACTION: seek out more information and use it to take steps toward improving your life, job, relationships—whatever it may be. To achieve the changes you want, you must educate yourself further and put in the work. Let me give you an example of how I convey this to my techs.

I often share this story with my technician when they are showing signs of stagnation. One thing all my techs have in common, no matter where they fall within their peers, is they all want to be better. The story I tell them, especially those who are struggling, is they won't wake up one morning and suddenly be twice as successful without effort. They magically aren't going from the bottom to the top. They are in control and no outside source is going to catapult them. They need to change, something. They need to educate themselves, talk to other technicians who excel, and gain the knowledge needed to improve. They must take action! Without it, they will remain static.

I urge them to change something! Doing the same thing the same way every day and expecting different results is insanity. It won't lead to positive changes for them, you, me or anybody else. In fact, staying stagnant can have the opposite effect, causing anger, resentment, laziness, and a host of other issues from the monotony. When you see others around you gaining traction and advancing while you remain stagnant, negative self-talk can start to creep in. As soon as I see it, in myself or one of my guys, I take steps to correct it. Our market is very successful because all my techs and I are in a constant state of improvement and are supportive of each other. So, take that first step, seek out knowledge, and make the changes necessary to move forward.

I guarantee you that all my techs are tired of hearing "Nothing Changes When Nothing Changes!" I say it every day, multiple times a day because it needs to sink in. Change only happens when you put in the effort to make it happen. That effort must involve gaining new knowledge so that when they face similar situations, they can act differently and improve from the last time. I've been lucky enough to see the light bulbs come on throughout the years, and when they do, the future is so exciting for those techs! That's why I get up every day trying to get my techs to see the light!

So, are we in agreement that you must take action to change something, add to your knowledge to improve and be more successful? I know that can be a lot to wrap your head around. It is for them sometimes. They think about change a lot. But I must remind them, thinking about change is NOT change. You have to take action.

Still a little foggy?

Here is one personal example of the action of gaining knowledge to becoming more successful: I know how to wire 110-volt outlets in houses. I can install lights, switches, and receptacles. I have that knowledge, but I'm by no means an electrician. One of the biggest tasks an electrician does is pull all the wiring in a house into a breaker box that takes electricity from the electric company's line and then distributes it throughout the house. I don't know how to do that. Following the principle of "Nothing Changes When Nothing Changes," I would have to educate myself on how to do it correctly and safely. I need to change my electrical knowledge, add to what I know, take action, and learn the steps to do that! Once I do, the change will occur and I will be more successful.

One more - A Mom's and Dad's parenting example: Imagine trying to potty train your toddler. You've tried everything—reward charts, songs, even promising a parade of their favorite cartoon characters. But nothing works. You've used every thought and process that you and your spouse have between you. You've used up all the knowledge you possess about getting the kid on the pot! You have even resorted to praying to the diaper genie in hopes real magic will happen. But alas, the day comes and you realize that just hoping your toddler will magically understand isn't going to cut it. You need to change your approach. So you start researching effective potty training methods, talking to other parents who have successfully navigated this milestone, and maybe even consulting a parenting expert. Armed with new knowledge, you introduce a fun, consistent routine, and suddenly, progress is being made. By changing your approach and gaining the right knowledge, you achieve the change you were hoping for. See? Even in parenting, nothing changes when nothing changes!

I know a large portion of you might think that everyone should naturally understand and grasp these concepts without much problem. I did also. However, over time and through personal experience, I've learned that this isn't the case. Many people must be taught these things. Far too many people believe that change will just happen, that things will just get better, and life will improve simply by thinking about it. Thinking about it over and over. Just like my techs think they will one day be at the top of the leader board by just waking up and taking no action. I hate to tell both groups: Not going to happen! This is one of the biggest lies we tell ourselves, and I have been guilty of it too. It's called Wishful Thinking. Wishful thinking gets you nowhere and improves nothing. I have volumes of personal disasters that all revolve around wishful thinking. Most people do. The cliches abound on this subject! Take your pick:

"Hope is not a strategy."

"Wishing won't make it so."

"Dreams don't work unless you do."

"You can't wish your way to success."

"Hoping for the best without preparing for the worst."

"Faith without works is dead."

QUIZ: Can you think of another word that describes this inaction? Yes, the second killer P: procrastination.

See how wishful thinking and inaction tie together to murder success and positive forward movement? It's amazing the damage it can do and you don't even know it's happening most of the time. Plus, wishful thinking can lead to some pretty bad decision-making. When we're not thinking critically, we overlook important details, which can lead to poor outcomes. It also makes us procrastinate, hoping things will magically get better without us doing anything. This mindset can make us avoid tough truths and miss out on opportunities.

Conversely we know Nothing changes when Nothing Changes and you Only Know What you Know put together mean you must take action to start the change! Change, success and improvement take action to happen, Not just thinking about it.

I would be remiss if I didn't acknowledge that sometimes things can improve without action. Winning the lottery, for instance, although you still had to take the action of buying a ticket. Another example is inheriting something from a family member or benefiting from the generosity of others. While these instances can lead to positive changes, they are not the norm by any stretch of the imagination. You are in charge of you own positive changes.

So, if you haven't recently won the lottery to improve your situation, you're just like the other millions of us. We will have to do the work. I hope you get the picture. You need to seek out the knowledge and put in the effort to become proficient. Take action! Get it? Knowledge truly is power! "Nothing Changes When Nothing Changes" and the "change" here is all about gaining knowledge and applying it. I know it seems that I have beaten this concept to death. Some of you might be thinking, "OK, we get it! Move on already!" Believe me, I understand. I have to be sure you get this. I've been in your shoes. For a long time, I heard "Nothing Changes When Nothing Changes" repeatedly, but it didn't truly click until much later in life. The two Killer P's—Procrastination and Patience (lack of)—had a strong hold on me. I kept waiting for change to happen on its own, but it never did. It wasn't until I decided to actively seek out knowledge and put in the effort that things began to shift. Imagine you're in a situation where every day feels like a repeat of the last. You wake up, go through the motions, and at the end of the day, nothing has changed. Even after thinking about it, really, really hard! It's frustrating, right?

That's the very essence of insanity—doing the same thing over and over again and expecting different results. To break out of this cycle, you must seek out new information, learn from others who have been successful, and apply that knowledge to your own life. So, as we move forward, remember this fundamental truth: Nothing Changes When Nothing Changes. It might seem repetitive, but it's a lesson worth repeating until it sinks in! Are we in agreement that to improve and be more successful, you must take action to change something? AMEN!

Now, let's talk about one final crucial piece of the change equation: in the powerful "WHY" chapter. Here it is: *"Accountability is the catalyst for change."* Up to this point you've recognized the need for change, understood that Nothing Changes When Nothing Changes, and committed to educating yourself. Now it's time to make yourself accountable. Yes, accountability! Accountability significantly boosts your chances of following through on your commitments. When you make yourself accountable, especially by sharing your goals with someone you respect—whether it's your spouse, a friend, your pastor, your boss, or a coworker—you deepen your commitment. Knowing that someone will check on your progress makes you more motivated to take action and complete your goals. Having an accountability partner provides support and encouragement, helping you stay focused and disciplined. This dynamic fosters continuous learning and improvement, making it more likely for you to stick to your plans and achieve your objectives. I wasn't always good at this. For a long time, my lack of accountability held me back. I thought I could do it all on my own, but I was wrong. Once I decided to hold myself accountable and share my goals with others, the path to success opened up for me. In essence, sharing your goals and making yourself accountable ingrains these commitments much deeper than merely thinking about them. This doesn't require a serious discussion or a formal contract. A brief conversation will suffice. Say the words out loud to another person.

By doing so, you not only clarify your intentions but also set the stage for real, actionable change. Remember, accountability is a powerful tool that keeps you on track and moving forward toward your goals. Accountability changed my life, and it can change yours too. It's the key to turning your intentions into actions and your dreams into reality. Think of accountability as your personal motivator, ensuring that your goals aren't just dreams but realities.

At its core, accountability is about accepting responsibility for your actions and being answerable to yourself and others for your decisions. It's about owning your tasks, being transparent about your progress and setbacks, and being ready to explain and justify your actions. Studies have shown that people who are held accountable for their actions tend to perform better. Knowing that your progress is being monitored encourages you to put in more effort and strive for higher standards. It helps build self-discipline because you have to consistently follow through on your commitments. This reinforces the habit of sticking to your plans and making necessary adjustments when challenges arise. Moreover, accountability fosters personal growth. It provides you with constructive feedback, helping you learn, grow, and develop new skills and strategies. Being accountable shows reliability and integrity. It tells others that you are responsible and trustworthy, which can strengthen your personal and professional relationships. When you're accountable, you're more likely to address problems head-on and find solutions. The need to report on progress pushes you to overcome obstacles rather than avoid them. Accountability is a powerful tool for driving significant change. It boosts your motivation, provides structure, enhances performance, and promotes personal growth. By making accountability a part of the change/success process, you can greatly increase your chances of achieving meaningful and lasting success. Embrace it as a key component of your journey toward improvement, change, and success. A catalyst is anything or anyone that causes a significant change or brings about an event or transformation. Accountability truly is the catalyst for change.

As with everything we have discussed, start small, if this is new to you. No need to lay out your entire life plan to a friend. For example, just let them know you are trying to get better at time management by using an on-line scheduling assistant. When you follow through and update them later, the feeling of success will be overwhelming and motivating. That will keep you going with being accountable. It is an amazing feeling! This is probably the most daunting concept I've shared so far, but it is also the most crucial. Honestly, this is where failure often occurs, and this is where quitting happens.

Quitting at this step in the process of change can lead to a cycle that repeats over and over again. I know that for myself, and probably for some of you, we've been stuck in this cycle. We have all the good intentions in the world. We recognize what needs to change, we start gathering the knowledge to make it happen, but then we don't follow through because it gets a little too difficult, we get impatient, we procrastinate. We tell ourselves, who is going to know that we didn't do it, we didn't follow through? No one. No harm, no foul. We quit and move on. I have been there and done that more times than I care to count. Do it long enough and you get to add shame to the mix! That can lead to more things we don't complete....on and on. The cycle has started, and it is devastating.

The good news is Accountability will jerk you from that cycle so that forward momentum can start. We are all different, of course. There are many reasons why you might not follow through, but for me, the biggest reason was a lack of accountability. I never told anyone about my plans for change or my goals for success. I'll say it again. You can break the quitting cycle by starting with just a little bit of accountability. Tell someone about your plans and let them help you stay on track. My lack of accountability was absolutely what stopped me from being successful and moving forward in my life. If I could give you a gift right now, wave a magic wand, and bestow upon you one powerful ability, it would be the ability to make yourself accountable.

Everything we've discussed up to this point is extremely important. You need to understand all the concepts; they aren't that difficult, but they all work together. I hope you see that accountability is the true catalyst for change. It's what takes all the other principles and turns them into real, meaningful transformation. It's the force that drives change, morphs your actions into results, and makes progress happen. Accountability. Embrace it and watch how it transforms your life.

To wrap up this chapter, let's take a step back and see the big picture. So far, we've delved into "Nothing Changes When Nothing Changes" with the "who," "what," "when," and "where." Now we've tackled the "why"—the heart of Part 1. We've explored why change is essential, how I've navigated it, and how I've seen it work wonders for others. Change is all about transforming and modifying, and success can be as varied as the people striving for it. From small victories to major achievements, it's the journey and the growth that matter. I wrote this book to share the strategies that have worked for me and others, and I believe they can work for you too.

Here's the kicker: Nothing changes when nothing changes. It's simple common sense. Whether you're rewiring your life or cooking up something new, knowledge and action are key. Oh, and don't forget the secret ingredient—accountability! Sharing your goals and having someone to answer to can make all the difference. So, are we ready to embrace change and accountability? Let's do this! Remember, even small steps can lead to big transformations. Now, let's move forward with enthusiasm and make those changes happen! The next two chapters mark the beginning of actionable steps with a strong emphasis on education. Chapters 6 and 7 are critical skills to practice and learn. They may be old hat to some of you and completely new to others. Either way, I think it would be a disservice not to at least touch on them before moving on. So, let's dive into the practical side of things and start transforming our lives one step at a time. Together, we'll turn the page to a new chapter of growth and success. Let's make those changes happen!

Preview Chapters 6 and 7

Chapter 6 talks about opportunities and how to capture them. A lot of people don't know how to spot opportunities, and as a result, they miss out on potential successes. This chapter will help you develop the mindset and skills needed to identify and evaluate opportunities and give you steps to take advantage of them effectively. We'll explore how to stay proactive, trust your instincts, and leverage your network to turn opportunities into tangible successes.

Chapter 7 is all about resilience—bouncing back from life's inevitable face-plants. It argues that setbacks aren't the end of the world; they're just detours on your way to awesomeness. Adopt a growth mindset: think of challenges as opportunities, not personal vendettas from the universe. Practical tips include setting small, achievable goals to boost your confidence, taking care of your health (yes, you need sleep), and practicing mindfulness to keep your cool. Look at J.K. Rowling and Steve Jobs—they faced epic fails and still came out on top. Resilience isn't just about surviving; it's about thriving and turning every setback into a slingshot that propels you forward. Embrace the bumps, learn from them, and keep moving forward with a smile.

These two chapters are essential because they provide the strategies and tools you need to take the insights from the first part of the book and turn them into real-world success. Think of them as your prep work before diving into the hands-on actionable items in Part Two. With a solid understanding of opportunities and the 'Oh Shit's', your ready to rock!

6

Chapter 6: Opportunities

Opportunities are like hidden gems scattered throughout our lives. Some people seem to stumble upon them effortlessly, while others struggle to recognize them even when they are right in front of them. This chapter aims to shed light on how to identify opportunities, evaluate their potential, and take steps to capitalize on them for success.

I have this formatted a little differently so it can be easily referenced. I'm hoping you come back here to reference some of this chapter when you have an inkling an opportunity is knocking. At the end of the chapter, I share a true story about one of the many opportunities that have presented themselves to me over the years. This is one I actually acted on very quickly. But first, the opportunity education.

Recognizing Opportunities

Opportunities often disguise themselves as hard work or challenges. Thomas Edison famously said, "Opportunity is missed by most people because it is dressed in overalls and looks like work." This means that opportunities may not always present themselves in obvious or attractive ways. Instead, they may require effort, perseverance, and a willingness to embrace challenges.

One of the first steps in recognizing opportunities is to maintain a positive and open mindset. If you focus on the positive aspects of situations and look for ways to turn challenges into opportunities, you will be better equipped to spot them. Additionally, trust your instincts. Often, our gut feelings can guide us toward recognizing chances that may not be immediately obvious.

Another key element is to be proactive. Rather than waiting for opportunities to come to you, actively seek them out. Identify areas in your life where you want to create change and take deliberate steps to make it happen. This could involve learning new skills, expanding your network, or stepping out of your comfort zone.

The Litmus Test for a Good Opportunity

Not every opportunity is worth pursuing. To determine if an opportunity is good, consider its potential benefits and how it aligns with your long-term goals. Evaluate the risks involved and weigh them against the potential rewards. Does the opportunity align with your values and goals? If it resonates with your core beliefs and contributes to your overall mission, it is likely worth pursuing. Lastly, consider whether the opportunity is feasible. Do you have the necessary resources, time, and skills to take advantage of it? If not, what steps can you take to acquire them?

Steps to Capitalize on Opportunities

Once you've recognized a good opportunity and determined that it's worth pursuing, follow these steps to make the most of it:

- Set Clear Goals: Start by defining what you want to achieve. Write down your goals and be as specific and detailed as possible.

Break your goals down into smaller, manageable steps to avoid feeling overwhelmed.

· Create a Detailed Plan: Identify the resources you will need, set deadlines, and establish milestones to track your progress. A well-thought-out plan acts as a road map, guiding you toward your objectives and helping you stay on track.

· Take Action: Begin by taking small, consistent steps toward your goal. Even minor progress can lead to significant results over time. The key is to keep moving forward, regardless of the pace.

· Stay Flexible: Be prepared to adapt your plans as circumstances change. Opportunities and situations are often dynamic, requiring you to adjust your strategies to stay on course.

· Network and Seek Support: Surround yourself with people who can offer advice, encouragement, and valuable insights. Networking opens doors to new possibilities and provides a wealth of knowledge from others who have walked similar paths.

· Reflect and Learn: Take time to reflect on your progress and learn from your experiences. What worked well? What could be improved? Use these reflections to refine your approach and continue growing. Continuous learning and adaptation are key to long-term success.

In my role at A1 Garage Door Service, I've seen how recognizing and seizing opportunities can lead to remarkable success. For instance, technicians who identify opportunities for bettering a KPI , (Key Performance Indicator) by further training often advance more quickly and perform better than those who don't. In addition, the ones that see these opportunities on their own do much better than the ones that are told about a possible opportunity. By actively seeking out these opportunities and committing to their growth, they open up new career possibilities and achieve their professional goals. Some techs actively look for these opportunities every day in the garage with the customers and are very successful. I tell all my techs: "Do what's right by the customer and everything else will follow." You can use that in every area of your life. Do what is right and opportunities will present themselves. I do believe that.

Recognizing and capitalizing on opportunities is a skill that can be developed with practice and the right mindset. By staying positive, being proactive, trusting your instincts, and carefully evaluating potential opportunities, you can position yourself for success. Remember, the key to making the most of opportunities lies in taking consistent, deliberate action toward your goals. With determination and perseverance, you can turn challenges into stepping stones and achieve the success you desire. An opportunity I saw and grabbed! As promised, here's the story of Building First Impressions—a whirlwind opportunity that presented itself to me many years ago. I have to admit, I didn't follow many of the rules above. The entire situation moved very fast!

Building first impressions.

Over two decades ago, I was living in Denver with my wife and our four young children. At the time, I didn't have a job, and our finances were tighter than a drum, but we had a lot of love, animals, and dreams. We lived in a house that my mother-in-law had generously bought for us. It wasn't much, but it was a roof over our heads. Being a handy guy, I had a few tools. I had recently been working in the industrial maintenance field at a well-known brick company in Denver, but I had lost that job due to some medical issues. One of those tools was a small power washer that my mother-in-law probably bought for us to clean something around the house. I didn't use it much, but I had it. One day, I had to go downtown to take care of some legal matters with my youngest son, who was about six at the time. As we moved through several buildings, I noticed a terrible smell at the entranceway—human poop and pee were everywhere. I thought, "Why isn't anyone cleaning these? It can't be that difficult." It was really gross and overwhelming. At that point in my life, my brain never turned off; I was always looking for an opportunity, honestly. That's when it hit me—"I could do this."

So, without hesitation, I went straight to the security desk of one of the buildings we had just left and asked if building management was on-site. They were, and they directed me to Mrs. Smith, the building manager, on the 10th floor. I remember it well. I told my son David to keep quiet and look cute. If I could duplicate the face he made when I said that, you would laugh for a week. David is, was, and always will be a character of all characters. He comes by it honestly. We walked into the outer office, and a secretary took us into Mrs. Smith's office almost directly. After a minute of pleasantries, she asked how she could help "two stunningly good-looking men." I blushed, and David giggled. I was direct and came to the point as business-like as I could in Levi 501s and Reebok high-tops. I asked if they had anyone cleaning the outer entranceway and mentioned the awful smells David and I experienced. She said they had a company that came occasionally, but she wasn't sure when they would next be around. She actually apologized to us, and I believe she thought that was the end of the conversation. I think she thought we had just come to see her to complain. I paused a second after her apology, smiled, and saw my chance. I told her I had a business that specializes in cleaning entranceways, and the name "Building First Impressions" popped into my head right there, and I blurted it out. I could see she was thinking about the name and smiling, and she said, "That is very clever." She asked how much I charged. On the spot, I came up with a reasonable number and suggested a bi-monthly service. She smiled again and almost looked relieved. She hired me immediately and asked when I could start. I told her I could begin within the week. So, in less than 15 minutes, I went from not having a job to having a job—a business as a matter of fact—and the wheels started turning. A week later, I brought my small power washer to her building, found a hose bib outside, and got to work. The job was tougher than I had expected, but when I finished, the entranceway looked spotless and smelled great. My wife had helped me devise a plan to clean and gave me some cleaner that had a pleasant aroma. That same day, after finishing her entranceway, I took an invoice I had printed from my computer the night before up to Mrs. Smith and asked if they could pay quickly since I needed to buy some supplies. She was happy to write me a check right then and there. With that first check, I bought a better power washer—a powerful 3500 PSI model. And just like that, Building First Impressions was born.

I share this story not as a step-by-step guide to starting a power washing business but to illustrate the importance of recognizing the skills and materials you have that others might need. When I woke up that morning, I had no idea what the day would bring. It all unfolded as I went about my business in downtown Denver. The key takeaway is to be aware of your surroundings, your skill set, and the needs of others. Now, earlier I mentioned that we had been in and out of two or three buildings that day, and all of them had the same problem. On my next visit to the same building, two people approached me and asked if I could do similar work for their buildings. Within a month, I had contracts to clean and power wash the entranceways of four different buildings twice a month. Word spread, and soon I was being asked to clean the exteriors of entire buildings. At one point, I even had to get a city permit to block off half of a downtown Denver street to power wash the first two stories of a 15-story building, renting scissor lifts and ladders to get the job done. So, remember, sometimes the best opportunities come from the most unexpected places. Keep your eyes open, your mind sharp, and never be afraid to seize the moment!

Another crucial lesson from this story is the importance of seizing opportunities without hesitation. I didn't overthink it or go home to ponder my next move. I saw an opportunity and acted on it immediately. That's where some greatness begins—recognizing and capitalizing on opportunities as they arise. I had the willingness to change on a dime. Sometimes that is what it takes. The accountability portion came without me even knowing what I was doing. I promised Mrs. Smith that I would clean the entranceway, and I did!

We all have moments when we look back and wish we had acted differently when an opportunity presented itself. In this instance, I seized the moment, and it worked out. After about a year, I had to sell all those contracts to another power washing company because I couldn't keep the business going due to some health issues. However, I sold those contracts, proving the value of acting on an opportunity when it comes your way. Stay alert, keep an open mind; you never know what might fall in your lap.

7

Chapter 7: Building Resilience and Overcoming Setbacks

Okay, so far, we've covered everything about moving forward, achieving success, getting better, and making positive personal changes. But before we dive into those actionable items, we need to do a 180° turn and talk about setbacks, failures, and resilience—how to see them coming and how to work through them.

When people are moving along a solid forward track and suddenly hit a wall, the tendency is often to throw up their hands and quit. I don't know the exact percentage, but it's got to be pretty high. Setbacks and failures are not negative; they're absolutely positive. They give us all the information we need about how not to do something. So take this chapter as seriously as you have all the rest because it will prepare you for when things don't go quite as planned.

First off, let's talk about resilience. Resilience isn't just a fancy word; it's that unshakable quality that allows you to bounce back from adversity and keep pushing forward, even when things get tough. It's like that old toy we had as kids—the inflatable clown you could punch, and it would pop right back up. Life's going to throw punches, and resilience is what ensures you pop back up every single time. Without resilience, even the best-laid plans can fall apart at the first sign of trouble.

Common setbacks can range from job losses and health issues to burnout and personal failures. All of which I have experienced. These setbacks can feel like a punch in the gut, but they don't have to derail you. The key is to see them for what they are: temporary obstacles, not insurmountable barriers. It's all about perspective. When you hit a wall, don't see it as the end of the road. See it as a challenge to find a new path, a new way forward.

So, how do you build resilience? It starts with your mindset. Adopt a growth mindset, where you view challenges as opportunities for growth, not as threats. When something goes wrong, instead of asking "Why is this happening to me?" ask "What can I learn from this?" This shift in perspective can turn every setback into a stepping stone toward your goals. It's about seeing the silver lining in every cloud, no matter how stormy it looks. I am the youngest of four children. Over 30 years ago my sister Charryn, the oldest, shared a piece of wisdom with me: "There is a positive in every negative; it's a law of the universe. For every action, there is a reaction." For some reason, I really took those words to heart and thought about them every time something 'bad' happened. Charryn passed away from breast cancer years ago, but her words have helped me get through some very challenging times. Thank you, Charryn.

Let's dive into some practical strategies. One of the most effective ways to build resilience is through small, consistent actions that boost your mental and emotional strength. Start by setting small, achievable goals. These mini-wins build your confidence and give you a sense of progress, even when the bigger picture feels overwhelming. And don't forget to take care of yourself—physically, emotionally, and mentally. Regular exercise, healthy eating, and adequate sleep are the foundations of a resilient mind and body.

Another powerful tool is mindfulness. It's not just a buzzword; it's a practice that can help you stay grounded and focused, even in the face of adversity. Spend a few minutes each day in meditation or simply being present in the moment. This can help you manage stress, stay calm, and maintain clarity when things get tough. It's like having a personal reset button that you can hit whenever you need to clear your mind and refocus your energy.

Think about people who have faced immense challenges and come out stronger on the other side. Take J.K. Rowling, who was rejected by multiple publishers before Harry Potter became a global phenomenon. Or Steve Jobs, who was fired from his own company only to return and revolutionize the tech industry. These stories aren't just feel-good tales; they're real-life examples of resilience in action. They show us that setbacks are not the end, but rather a crucial part of the journey to success.

Resilience isn't just about bouncing back. It's about bouncing forward. It's using every setback as a slingshot, propelling you further than you were before. It's about growing stronger with each challenge, learning more, and becoming more determined. It's about developing a relentless spirit that refuses to be broken.

Building resilience is a lifelong process. It's about continuously developing the mental toughness to face whatever comes your way. As you build this resilience, you'll find that setbacks become less daunting. They're no longer roadblocks but rather detours that lead you to new and often better paths. Practice. Now, let's talk about accountability again. That word keeps popping up because it's crucial, not just for making positive strides forward, but also for dealing with setbacks. Accountability isn't only about celebrating wins; it's equally important when something goes wrong. Don't keep your failures to yourself—share them with someone, process what happened, and if you're confident enough, explain where you think you went wrong and what you would do differently next time. A person who keeps all their failures to themselves is likely to repeat the same mistakes over and over. I'm not saying that's true for everyone because there are certainly people who have failed in silence and then moved on to bigger, better things. However, I would bet that they felt pretty lonely during that process. Sharing your failures can be just as beneficial as sharing your triumphs. It's about learning, growing, and moving forward with a clearer understanding of what needs to change. Accountability works both ways for me, and I've seen it work for many of my technicians. Our owner, Tommy Mello, is a perfect example. On more than one occasion, he has shared his failures with the entire company during meetings. He doesn't shy away from letting us know what went wrong and how he plans to avoid those mistakes in the future. By doing this, Tommy not only learns from his experiences but also sets an example for the rest of us. He shows that it's okay to fail as long as you're willing to be accountable and learn from those failures. This transparency makes him a better leader and a better man. So, whether it's a triumph or a failure, accountability is key. It helps you process your experiences, learn from them, and ultimately become more successful. Keep this in mind as you move forward— embrace accountability in all its forms and watch how it transforms your journey.

Take this chapter to heart. Embrace the bumps and hurdles as part of the journey. Use the strategies we've discussed to build your resilience muscle. And get ready to tackle the actionable steps in Part Two with a renewed sense of strength and determination. The road to success isn't always smooth, but with resilience, you can navigate it with confidence and grace. Let's keep pushing forward, no matter what.

As we wrap up Part 1 of "Nothing Changes When Nothing Changes," let's take a moment to reflect on the journey we've embarked upon. We've delved into the foundational concepts of change, understanding the "who," "what," "when," "where," and "why" behind it. We've discussed the importance of recognizing the need for transformation, the power of knowledge, and the critical role of accountability. These principles are not just theoretical—they are the bedrock upon which real, lasting change is built. With a solid grasp of these concepts, we are now ready to move forward.

In "Nothing Changes When Nothing Changes," the next part of our journey will be a road map filled with actionable items and practical strategies that will help you apply these principles to your life. Get ready to dive into concrete steps and hands-on exercises designed to propel you toward meaningful and sustainable change. Let's move forward with confidence and enthusiasm, turning insights into actions and dreams into reality.

Welcome to Part 2: The Journey of Transformation Continues with Actionable Insights and Practical Guidance.

Afterword

As I sit down to write this, I can't help but smile at how fitting it is that *"Nothing Changes When Nothing Changes"* is the culmination of all the years I've known the author. If there's anyone who embodies the idea that change is the key to growth, it's him. I've had the privilege of witnessing his journey—both as a friend and a colleague—and I can tell you firsthand, this book is a true reflection of the way he lives and leads.

What's remarkable about the author is that he doesn't just talk about change—he embraces it, and he inspires everyone around him to do the same. Whether it's tackling a new challenge at work or pushing his team to think differently, his energy is always focused on improvement. I've seen it time and time again—when something isn't working, he doesn't complain, he makes adjustments. It's that simple for him: you either change, or you stay stuck. And trust me, "stuck" is not a word he's comfortable with!

The personal stories in this book aren't just words on a page—they're real, lived experiences. I've seen how applying these principles can turn around, not just a project or a quarter, but entire careers. The way he's woven those experiences into practical, actionable steps is classic JD—always wanting to share what he's learned, to help others succeed.

I can tell you, working with the author has been a masterclass in adaptability. He has taught all of us that waiting for change to come to you isn't enough—you have to seek it out, initiate it, and be ready to ride the wave of whatever comes next. What stands out the most, though, is that no matter how high he climbs, he never loses sight of helping others do the same. That's what makes this book special—

it's not just about his journey; it's a guide for anyone who wants to transform their own life.

As you finish this book, know that the advice given here comes from someone who genuinely wants you to succeed. It's not just theory—it's lived, it's tested, and it works. The truth is, nothing really changes until you make the decision to act, and this book is the roadmap for doing just that. If you take one thing away from all of this, let it be the courage to make that first move, no matter how small.

To the author—thank you for leading by example and showing all of us that change is not something to fear, but something to chase. This book is just the beginning for the readers, but for those of us who know you, it's the culmination of the mindset you've been living and teaching all along. Here's to many more changes—and the successes that come with them.

Luke Martin
COO A1 Garage Door Service

Part 2

Introduction

Welcome to Part 2 of "Nothing Changes When Nothing Changes." If you've made it this far, you're ready to dive deeper and build on the foundation we laid in Part 1. In the first part, we explored the personal side of change—why it's necessary, the mindset shifts needed, and the importance of understanding that nothing changes when nothing changes. These concepts are not just theories but practical tools I've used throughout my life and career to foster growth and success. Part 1 was about setting the stage, understanding the fundamental principles, and getting into the right mindset.

Now, in Part 2, we're shifting gears to focus on actionable steps and strategies to drive meaningful change in your life. This section is designed to be a practical manual—a step-by-step guide filled with detailed instructions, strategies, and insights to help you implement the concepts we discussed in Part 1. Change! We'll explore various areas of life where change can make a significant impact, from building discipline and setting SMART goals to recognizing and seizing opportunities.

In the early chapters, you'll learn about building a solid morning routine, setting SMART goals, mastering time management techniques, and creating healthy habits. These initial steps lay the groundwork for productivity and long-term health. Moving midway through, we'll tackle overcoming procrastination, enhancing effective communication skills, building resilience, and the importance of networking and relationship building. These chapters provide strategies to maintain focus, bounce back from setbacks, and create valuable connections.

Later chapters will delve into managing stress, practical financial planning advice, embracing continuous learning, and the importance of regularly reflecting and adjusting your path. These topics ensure you maintain mental health, manage your finances wisely, and continue to grow personally and professionally. Each chapter in this part is packed with information you can refer to over and over again. Whether you're looking to improve your morning routine, develop better habits, overcome procrastination, or manage stress, you'll find the tools and techniques you need here. Consider Part 2 as your go-to resource, your playbook for advancing towards success. It's more than just advice; it's a collection of tried-and-true methods that have helped countless individuals, including myself, achieve their goals and transform their lives. These sections are fast, furious, and packed with action items. I don't drone on and on about any one subject. You'll find enough information to decide if it's something you want to use. If you like it, go ahead and use it, and then dig deeper on your own if you want. I wanted to give you as many choices as possible, all in one place.

So, get ready to take notes, highlight key points, and revisit these chapters whenever you need a boost or a reminder of the path you're on. Let's continue this journey together, making every step count towards building a better, more successful future.

Part 2

Chapter 1: Building a Foundation for Discipline

Alright, let's cut to the chase. Discipline isn't just a fancy word your gym teacher shouted while making you run laps; it's the core ingredient in the recipe for success. Think of it as the secret sauce that transforms an ordinary dish into a gourmet meal. Now, who wouldn't want a taste of that? In this chapter, we're going to start with the fundamentals, the bedrock upon which you can build a fortress of success. And it all begins the moment you open your eyes to greet the new day.

1.1 Morning Routines That Fuel Success

Have you ever noticed how a well-oiled machine doesn't hesitate? It just powers on, doing what it's designed to do. That's kind of the vibe we're going for with your morning routine. But here's the kicker: there's no one-size-fits-all approach here. What revs up one person might totally flop for another. So, let's talk about crafting a morning routine that's more tailored than a bespoke suit and why it's absolutely crucial to kick-start your day with intention.

Establishing a Purposeful Start

Imagine the most successful folks you know or have read about. There's a good chance they start their day with purpose. Take tech moguls who meditate, athletes who hit the gym, or writers who scribble pages at dawn. It isn't just about the activities they choose; it's about setting a deliberate tone for the day. When you begin your day with a routine that aligns with your goals, you're not just biding time; you're strategically setting the stage for all the victories to come. It's like placing the first domino in a series, perfectly aligned to trigger a cascade of productivity and success.

Customizing Your Routine

Now, how do you carve out a morning routine that fits your life and ambitions like a glove? First, identify what feels most out of alignment in your current morning flow. Are you always rushed, skipping breakfast, or maybe diving straight into emails? Start by addressing these pain points. If calm is what you're after, consider meditation or journaling. If you need energy, a quick workout could be your golden ticket. The key is to experiment and tweak until you find a rhythm that feels right and resonates with your personal goals. Remember, your morning routine should energize you, not exhaust you. It should feel like putting on your favorite playlist, not like a chore list you dread.

The Impact of Consistency

Let's talk about consistency because it's the real game-changer. Consistency in your morning routine acts like compound interest in your bank account. The more you do it, the more it pays off. Psychologically, a consistent start reduces decision fatigue and mental clutter, setting a clear, unperturbed path for the day. It's about creating a reliable rhythm that signals to your brain, "Hey, it's go-time!" And before you know it, this consistency breeds more self-discipline across all areas of your life. It's like training a muscle; the more you use it, the stronger it gets.

Tools and Apps to Aid Routine Formation

In our tech-savvy world, why not leverage some digital assistants to keep your morning routine on track? Apps like "Habitica" gamify your daily habits, making consistency fun, or "Headspace" for guided morning meditations to clear your mind. Then there's "My Morning Routine," which allows you to customize and track routines to ensure you're hitting all your marks. These tools are here to serve as your personal accountability partners, providing nudges and stats that help you stay the course until, one day, you don't even think about it; you just do it.

So there you have it. Your morning ritual isn't just about getting up and out the door; it's about setting the tone for a disciplined, intentional day. Stay consistent, tailor your routine to fuel your goals, and let the tools available help you maintain your path. It's these morning moments that can, believe it or not, transform an ordinary day into an extraordinary one. And it all starts with you deciding to make the first move right after you shake off the sleep. Let's make every morning count.

1.2 The Science of Habit Formation: Building Blocks of Discipline

Let's crack open the code behind habit formation, a critical player in the theater of daily life and your personal transformation. Think of habits as the programming language of your brain, operating behind the scenes to influence your actions without the need for conscious thought. Understanding this process isn't just academic; it's like getting the cheat codes to the video game of life.

Understanding the Habit Loop

The concept of the habit loop was popularized by Charles Duhigg in his book "The Power of Habit." At its core, the habit loop consists of three elements: cue, routine, and reward. The cue triggers the routine, the routine is the behavior itself, and the reward is what your brain gets out of the routine, which reinforces the habit loop. For example, your alarm clock rings (cue), you brush your teeth (routine), and you feel a minty fresh zap of cleanliness (reward), making it more likely that you'll repeat the same action the next morning when the alarm rings. By recognizing the patterns that form your habits, you gain the power to change them. It's like seeing the matrix of your daily life and tweaking the parts that don't serve your ultimate goals.

Strategies to Form Good Habits

Transitioning from understanding to action, let's talk about shifting your habits. The key here is to start small. If you aim to transform from a night owl into an early bird, don't set a 5 AM alarm right away. Instead, wake up just 15 minutes earlier than usual, and gradually adjust. This method reduces resistance. It's akin to heating the frog slowly; it doesn't realize the change until it's already happening. Consistency here is your best friend. Perform your new routine at the same time each day to strengthen the new habit loop. And remember, patience and persistence are your allies. It typically takes about 66 days to form a new habit, not the 21 days of popular myth. So, commit to giving yourself time to adapt.

Role of the Environment in Habit Formation

Your environment plays a pivotal role in shaping your habits. It's like the stage setting for your daily performance. If you're trying to eat healthier, keep fruits and vegetables within easy reach and stash the junk food out of sight. The principle is simple: make good habits easier and bad habits harder. If your goal is to exercise more, lay out your workout clothes the night before, or keep your gym bag packed and ready. You're more likely to hit the gym if you reduce the friction to get started. Think of your environment as a garden; what you plant and nurture is what will grow. Cultivate an environment that supports the habits you want to flourish.

Long-term Benefits of Solid Habits

The cultivation of solid habits doesn't just make your daily life easier; it also sets the foundation for long-term success and personal growth. Good habits, like saving a small part of your paycheck each month, compound over time, leading to financial security. Regular, moderate exercise can improve your health, reducing medical costs and keeping you active and able in your later years. Over time, what starts as a simple routine becomes a cornerstone of your life strategy. These habits act like automatic gears driving you towards your goals, even when your motivation fluctuates. In the grand scheme, the strength and resilience you develop from good habits ripple out to all facets of your life, reinforcing your ability to tackle any challenge that comes your way.

In wrapping up this section, remember that each small habit you form and maintain is a testament to your commitment to personal excellence. Think of them as individual bricks in the fortress you are building. Each one is fundamental, each one matters, and together, they form a formidable structure that defines the landscape of your life.

1.3 Overcoming Procrastination with Cognitive Behavioral Techniques

Procrastination: the art of putting off until tomorrow what you could (and should) absolutely get done today. It's a common adversary for many of us, and let me tell you, it's as sneaky as they come. It whispers sweet nothings like "just five more minutes on social media," and before you know it, hours have zipped by, and you're in a panic. The good news? It's beatable. By understanding the psychological triggers and employing a few clever strategies, you can kick procrastination to the curb. Let's roll up our sleeves and tackle this beast together.

Identifying Triggers

First off, recognizing the triggers is like playing detective in your own psychological thriller. Procrastination isn't about laziness; it's often about underlying fears—fear of failure, fear of not being perfect, or even fear of success. For example, let's say you've been putting off starting a big project. Deep down, there might be a nagging doubt about your abilities, a lurking fear that you won't do it well. Or maybe, it's a monotonous task that you find utterly unstimulating. By identifying these triggers, you can start to understand what's really holding you back. It's about asking the right questions: What about this task makes me uncomfortable? What am I really avoiding here? Is it the task itself, or is it my feelings about the task?

Cognitive Restructuring

Once those sneaky triggers are out in the open, it's time for some cognitive restructuring—a fancy term for changing your thought patterns. Negative thinking can chain you down like an anchor. Cognitive restructuring is about turning those heavy, leaden thoughts into something lighter and more buoyant. Let's say you're thinking, "I must do this perfectly, or it's a complete failure." That's a heavy thought, right? Re-frame it to, "I'll do my best, and that's good enough." See, much lighter! This technique involves observing your thoughts, challenging them, and replacing them with more rational, supportive ones. It's like performing a software update on your brain's default settings.

Setting Micro-Goals

Now, onto the action part—setting micro-goals. This is about breaking your tasks down into bite-sized, less intimidating pieces. Imagine you're staring down a 20-page report. Instead of getting overwhelmed by the entirety of it, break it down: today, you'll outline the first two pages. Tomorrow, you'll research a specific part. By setting these micro-goals, the task becomes less daunting, more manageable, and hey, you might even find it enjoyable. Each small goal is a step on the staircase leading you to the completion of your project. It's about progress, not perfection.

Reward Systems

And speaking of steps, why not reward yourself for climbing them? Setting up a reward system can turbocharge your motivation. Completed your daily micro-goal? Great, take a break and watch an episode of your favorite series. Finished that daunting report? Treat yourself to a nice dinner or a new book. Rewards reinforce positive behavior, making it more likely you'll stick to your guns next time around. It's a bit like training a pet: do the trick, get a treat. Only in this case, you're both the trainer and the trained.

So, there you have it—procrastination isn't an invincible foe. With the right techniques, you can understand its origins, rewire your thinking, break tasks down to manageable sizes, and even make the process rewarding. It's about taking control, one thought, one action, one reward at a time. Now, let's get back to work, shall we? After all, those tasks won't complete themselves, no matter how long we stare at them!

1.4 Setting Realistic Goals and Milestones

Let's get real about goals. Not the "I want to be a millionaire by next Thursday" kind, but the real, tangible goals that you can actually see yourself achieving step by step. Setting goals is like planting seeds in your garden. You need to choose the right ones, plant them properly, and then nurture them until they blossom. That's where SMART goals come into play. SMART stands for Specific, Measurable, Achievable, Relevant, and Time-bound. It's a foolproof method to ensure your goals aren't just wishes.

SMART Goals: Detailing the Framework

Imagine you want to write a book, which seems like a mountain of a task. To make this goal SMART, start by specifying what kind of book—let's say it's a 300-page novel about a middle-aged, adventure-seeking archaeologist. Next, it needs to be measurable; decide how you'll measure progress, perhaps by aiming to write three pages a day. It should be achievable; ensure you have the time and resources to write daily. Make it relevant; this should be a goal that fuels your passion, not just something you think you should do. Lastly, set a time-bound plan; perhaps you aim to finish your first draft in 100 days. Suddenly, writing a book isn't just a vague dream, but a concrete plan that unfolds day by day.

Breaking Down Large Goals

Now, let's chop that big audacious goal into bite-sized pieces. It's like eating a steak—if you try to swallow it whole, you'll choke. But cut it into pieces, and it's a delightful meal. If your goal is to get fit, break it into phases. Phase one might be to walk 10,000 steps a day. Once that's a breeze, phase two could involve adding two days of weight training per week. Each phase builds on the last, making the overall goal more digestible and less intimidating. This method keeps motivation high, as you're not overwhelmed by the enormity of the task. Each small victory is a stepping stone to the next, keeping the momentum going strong.

Visualizing Success

Here's where it gets fun—visualization. This isn't just daydreaming; it's a potent tool used by athletes, entrepreneurs, and top performers worldwide. When you visualize achieving your goals, you're mentally and emotionally aligning yourself with the outcome. It's about seeing yourself crossing the finish line, feeling the sweat and the exhilaration. This mental rehearsal not only boosts motivation but also primes your brain to seize opportunities that align with your goals. It's like setting your internal GPS to the destination of success. Each day, spend a few minutes closing your eyes and vividly imagining reaching your milestones. Feel the success, the pride, and the joy. This practice will not only increase your desire to achieve the goal but also subconsciously guide your actions towards making it a reality.

Monitoring and Adjusting Goals

Life is what happens when you're busy making other plans, right? That's why monitoring and adjusting your goals is crucial. Think of it as being the captain of a ship. Sometimes the weather changes, and you need to adjust your course. Keep a regular check on your progress. Maybe every Sunday, review what you've accomplished towards your goals that week. This isn't just about ticking boxes; it's about reflective practice, seeing what worked, what didn't, and why. Maybe you planned to jog every morning, but it turns out you're not a morning person. No problem—try jogging in the evening. Adjusting your strategies isn't admitting defeat; it's tweaking your tactics to make sure you win the war, even if you lose a battle here and there.

Setting goals shouldn't be a dreary office task; it should be as alive and dynamic as you are. Using the SMART framework makes your goals clear and reachable. Breaking them down keeps them manageable. Visualizing them brings them closer to reality, and staying flexible ensures that you stay on track no matter what life throws at you. Remember, the goal is not just to dream, but to achieve.

1.5 The Role of Accountability Partners in Maintaining Discipline

When it comes to keeping your discipline on track, think of an accountability partner as your personal coach, cheerleader, and occasionally, the friendly referee who calls you out when you're about to foul. Choosing the right person for this role is more art than science, but get it right, and it's like finding gold. You want someone who's not only supportive but will also push you to achieve your best, even when you'd rather binge-watch the latest series on Netflix than review your budget or hit the gym.

Choosing the Right Accountability Partner

So, what should you look for? First off, find someone who shares or at least understands your goals and values. It's like picking a doubles partner in tennis; their game doesn't have to be a mirror image of yours, but it helps if you're both playing to win. They should be someone you respect—someone whose opinion you value and who you don't want to let down. This could be a colleague who's also climbing the career ladder, a friend who is passionate about personal development, or even a family member who's always had a knack for keeping you in check. The key is consistency and positivity. You need someone who will be as committed to your success as their own and can dish out tough love without being discouraging.

Structure of Accountability Relationships

Setting up the structure of this relationship is crucial. It's not just about catching up over coffee and calling it accountability. You need a system. Start by setting clear expectations. How often will you check in? What's the mode of communication? Will you meet in person, or can a video call suffice? Then, plan regular intervals for updates—daily, weekly, or bi-weekly, whatever suits your goals. During these check-ins, discuss not just what you've accomplished but also the hurdles you're facing. It's not a vent session, but a strategy meeting. You should leave each meeting with actionable feedback, feeling motivated, not just heard. And remember, this is a two-way street. You should be prepared to offer the same level of insightful, constructive feedback to your partner.

Digital Tools for Accountability

In today's world, there's no shortage of digital tools to keep you and your accountability partner connected. Platforms like Trello or Asana are great for tracking progress on specific projects or goals. They allow you to set up tasks, deadlines, and reminders, which both you and your partner can access and update. For habit tracking, apps like HabitShare blend personal accountability with social networking, letting you share your progress with friends. Then there's Coach.me, which provides not only tracking but also access to a community of coaches and peers who can offer guidance and motivation. These tools make the process of staying accountable less daunting and a lot more manageable.

Benefits of Peer Support

The benefits of having an accountability partner go beyond just keeping you on track. Psychologically, knowing that someone is rooting for you can enhance your motivation. It taps into our innate desire not to let others down, which can be a powerful motivator. Practically, regular check-ins provide opportunities to reflect on your progress, reassess goals, and tweak your approach. It's easy to get lost in the daily grind, but having a dedicated time to look at the bigger picture can be incredibly valuable. Plus, celebrating your wins with someone who understands the struggle can be hugely satisfying—it's not just your victory but a shared one.

So, whether you're trying to climb the corporate ladder, improve your health, or learn a new skill, having the right accountability partner can make the journey a lot smoother. It's about building a partnership that fosters mutual growth and success—a partnership where both of you are invested in seeing each other succeed. Remember, the right accountability partner not only keeps you focused and on track but also makes the path to achieving your goals a lot more enjoyable.

1.6 Evaluating Progress: Tools and Techniques for Self-Assessment

Let's talk about keeping an eye on the ball, or in our case, tracking the progress you're making. It's like having a personal scoreboard that shows not just the points you've scored but also highlights where you might need to up your game. This isn't about obsessive self-scrutiny that leaves you second-guessing every decision. Instead, it's about developing a keen sense of awareness regarding your growth, which is crucial for steering your ship in the right direction. Here, I'll share some of the most effective techniques for self-assessment and how they can transform the way you track your journey towards success.

Self-Monitoring Techniques

First up, let's look at the arsenal of tools at your disposal for self-monitoring. Journaling, for instance, is a powerhouse tool. It's like having a dialogue with yourself, where you lay out what you've done, how you felt about it, and what you think you could improve. It's not just about writing what you did each day; it's about reflecting on those actions and their impacts. This practice can provide profound insights into your behavioral patterns and emotional responses, helping you to fine-tune your actions moving forward.

Then there are apps—our digital companions that make tracking almost anything under the sun a breeze. Apps like Daylio allow you to track your mood and activities, helping you see correlations between what you do and how you feel. If you're more of a numbers person, try Toggl or RescueTime; they are fantastic for tracking how much time you spend on various tasks, giving you a clear picture of where your hours are going. Using these tools consistently allows you to gather data about yourself that can be incredibly eye-opening and, frankly, sometimes a bit surprising.

Quantitative vs. Qualitative Assessment

Now, diving a bit deeper, it's crucial to balance quantitative data with qualitative insights. Quantitative data—like hours spent on a task, money saved, or items crossed off a checklist—offers a bird's-eye view of your productivity and efficiency. It's straightforward and measurable, which is great for setting benchmarks and goals. However, this data doesn't always capture the full picture. That's where qualitative assessment comes into play. How satisfied are you with the progress? Are you feeling stressed or energized? This subjective data is critical as it helps you gauge the sustainability and enjoyment of your pursuits. Both types of data are necessary; they complement each other and provide a holistic view of your progress.

Adjusting Strategies Based on Feedback

Armed with this information, you're in a prime position to tweak and adjust your strategies. Let's say your data shows you're spending 40 hours a week on a project, but you're not making the kind of progress you'd hoped for. That's a cue to reassess your approach. Maybe you need to delegate, or perhaps it's about refining your workflow. Feedback, whether it comes from cold, hard data or your introspective journal entries, is invaluable. It acts as a course corrector, helping you to continually refine and optimize how you work and live. The goal here isn't to over-analyze but to stay responsive and adaptable, keeping your efforts aligned with your objectives.

Celebrating Milestones

Finally, let's not forget about celebrating your milestones. Recognition of your progress isn't just a nice pat on the back; it's an essential component of maintaining motivation. Whether it's a small win like sticking to your morning routine for a week, or a big one like landing a new client or finishing a project, take a moment to celebrate. These celebrations reinforce your successes, making the journey enjoyable and memorable. Plus, they serve as fuel for your next set of goals. Setting up small rewards for reaching milestones can keep things exciting and can be a great way to ensure you recognize and value your own hard work. Remember, every big achievement is a series of smaller victories.

Using these tools and techniques to monitor and adjust your progress is like having high-quality gauges in a car. They provide you with the necessary information to navigate effectively, making sure you're not just moving, but moving in the right direction. By taking the time to assess both the quantitative and qualitative aspects of your actions, adjusting your strategies based on this feedback, and celebrating your wins, you create a dynamic loop of continuous improvement. This isn't just about reaching your destination; it's about enjoying the ride and growing along the way.

Part 2

Chapter 2: Mastering Mental Toughness and Stress Management

Ever watched an athlete, sweat dripping, muscles tensing, a look of unwavering focus in their eyes, right before they smash a world record? There's something almost superhuman about it, isn't there? But here's a little secret: that ironclad mental toughness isn't just reserved for the sports elites. It's available to you and me, and it's more teachable and attainable than you might think. In this chapter, we're diving deep into the playbook of mental toughness, borrowing a few tactics from top athletes that you can apply to your daily grind, whether it's nailing a presentation, managing tight deadlines, or just juggling the chaos of everyday life.

Mental Toughness: Lessons from Elite Athletes

Adopting an Athlete's Mindset

Imagine stepping into the shoes of a pro athlete for a moment. Picture the discipline, the perseverance, the relentless pursuit of a goal. Now, what if you brought a slice of that mindset to your own challenges? Adopting an athlete's mindset means seeing every day as a training day. No elite athlete ever made it by going half-hearted into their training sessions, and the same goes for any personal or professional goal you might have. It's about setting your eyes on the prize with razor-sharp focus and pushing through the sweat and tears. Remember, discipline and perseverance aren't just about doing things when it feels good; it's about sticking to your game plan even when it feels like the last thing you want to do.

Training Routines for Mental Strength

Athletes don't just train their bodies; they train their minds. They engage in mental rehearsals before big events, picturing each step to victory, which you can do too. Before a major work presentation, visualize yourself delivering every point with confidence. Imagine the applause. Feel the satisfaction of nailing it. Techniques like these enhance focus and endurance, preparing you to handle the real thing with less anxiety and more confidence. Incorporate routine mental training exercises into your day, such as meditation or setting daily affirmations. Over time, these exercises strengthen your mental resilience, much like muscles bulking up after weeks of lifting weights.

Handling Pressure

Pressure, the old foe—we've all felt its weighty presence. Athletes face this giant head-on. Think of a basketball player at the free-throw line, the game's outcome resting on their shoulders. The secret to their cool demeanor? A cocktail of deep breathing, positive self-talk, and laser-like focus. You can apply these same techniques during high-stake business meetings or tight project deadlines. Practice controlled breathing to keep your physical response to stress in check, use positive affirmations to reinforce your capability, and focus entirely on the task at hand, blocking out the noise that tells you it's too much. It's about transforming pressure from a crippling adversary into a focusing energy.

Case Studies: Athletes Who Exemplify Mental Toughness

Let's take a page from the books of some sports legends. Consider Michael Jordan, known not just for his physical prowess but his mental game. His relentless practice routine, his ability to stay focused under pressure, and his refusal to be discouraged by failures (remember, he was once cut from his high school basketball team) underline the essence of mental toughness. Or Serena Williams, whose comeback stories are a testament to her mental fortitude, proving time and again that setbacks should be viewed as setups for greater comebacks. These athletes don't just train to win; they train to rebound from losses stronger than ever. Their stories are not just inspiring; they offer practical frameworks for cultivating resilience and a never-quit attitude.

By integrating these athlete-inspired strategies into your life, you not only boost your ability to handle everyday pressures but also enhance your capacity to achieve consistent success. It's about building a mindset that welcomes challenges, embraces adversity, and thrives under pressure—turning you into the MVP of your own life. So, lace up those mental sneakers, and let's hit the mental gym!

Mindfulness Techniques for Reducing Stress in High-Pressure Situations

Let's talk about mindfulness, a term that's been floating around like a leaf in the breeze in today's hyper-connected, always-on world. If you think it's just about sitting crossed-legged and humming to yourself, think again. Mindfulness is about being present, really present, in the moment. It's about observing your life as it unfolds without judgment, without reaching for your phone, and without rehashing the past or fretting about the future. This simple yet profound practice can slice through stress like a hot knife through butter, sharpen your focus, and significantly enhance your overall mental well-being. So, how exactly does this magic work?

First, let's break down the basic principle of mindfulness: attention. The core of mindfulness is learning to pay attention to your present experience, whether that's your breath, the sensations in your body, or the sounds around you. It sounds simple, but anyone who's tried to meditate knows that the mind is like a wild horse, galloping off in a million directions. The practice then becomes about gently bringing your attention back when it wanders, without beating yourself up about it. This act, repeated over and over, trains your brain to focus better, stay more alert, and remain calm under pressure.

Now, imagine you're in a high-stress situation—say, a looming deadline or a difficult conversation. Instead of your pulse racing and thoughts whirling like a storm, you can call on your mindfulness training to help stabilize your mind. Techniques like focused breathing or sensory observation can anchor you in the present, preventing stress from spiraling. Plus, this isn't just anecdotal; numerous studies back the effectiveness of mindfulness in reducing stress. Research shows that mindfulness meditation can decrease the density of brain tissue associated with anxiety and stress, and it can improve areas related to attention and emotional regulation.

Integrating mindfulness into your daily routine isn't about carving out two hours of zen time in a Himalayan cave; it's about small practices woven into your day. Start with a morning minute of mindfulness. Before you reach for your phone or coffee, spend sixty seconds noticing your breath or listening to the sounds around you. Turn routine activities, like showering or eating lunch, into mindful moments, focusing fully on the sensations and experiences. This doesn't just amplify your day with pockets of calm but also builds your mindfulness muscle, making it stronger day by day.

Let's dive a bit deeper with some quick and effective mindfulness exercises tailored for high-pressure environments. A favorite is the "Five Senses" exercise. Wherever you are, take a moment to notice five things you can see, four things you can hear, three things you can touch, two things you can smell, and one thing you can taste. This can be a quick circuit breaker in a stressful situation, redirecting your attention from anxiety to the present moment. Another great tool is the "Mindful Stop": S—Stop what you're doing, T—Take a breath, O—Observe your thoughts, body, and emotions, P—Proceed with intention. This can be a lifesaving pause that brings clarity and calmness in the eye of a storm.

Embracing mindfulness isn't about changing the waves that life throws at you; it's about learning to surf them. With practice, mindfulness not only lowers stress but also enhances your performance by keeping you concentrated and calm in the heat of the moment. Whether you're facing a tough decision, managing a hectic schedule, or simply need to focus in a noisy environment, mindfulness offers a toolkit for navigating life with greater ease and effectiveness. By cultivating a mindful approach, you prepare yourself to handle life's pressures not just adequately, but brilliantly.

Establishing Boundaries to Prevent Burnout

Let's talk about something as essential as your morning coffee but often as overlooked as the terms and conditions on software updates—boundaries. Why, you ask? Because without them, you're likely heading for a burnout faster than a cheap candle on a windy night. Boundaries are your personal guidelines, the lines in the sand that help you maintain not just your sanity but also your relationships and productivity. They're the unsung heroes in the narrative of your life, ensuring you don't spread yourself too thin or end up feeling like a doormat.

So, why are boundaries crucial for your mental health and stress management? Think of them as the psychological equivalent of airbags in cars. They cushion you against the impact of life's demands, protecting your time, energy, and emotional well-being.

Without these boundaries, it's easy to over-commit—be it to social gatherings, work projects, or even binge-watching sessions—which can lead to stress, resentment, and yes, the dreaded burnout. By defining what you are and aren't willing to tolerate, you not only safeguard your mental health but also foster a sense of self-respect and self-worth.

Now, setting these boundaries might sound as daunting as learning quantum physics overnight, but fear not. It's about being clear on what matters most to you and understanding your limits. Start simple. Communicate your needs clearly and effectively with colleagues, family, and friends. This might mean telling your team that you won't answer emails after 7 PM or letting your friends know that you need a day to yourself. The key here is consistency. The more consistently you enforce your boundaries, the more they are respected. Remember, people aren't mind readers, and they'll often test your limits not out of malice but simply because they don't know where the line is drawn.

But what happens when these well-set boundaries are challenged, as they inevitably will be? Here's where the art of assertiveness comes in. Being assertive doesn't mean being aggressive; it's about respecting yourself enough to ask for what you need while respecting others too. Say your boss regularly asks you to stay late. Instead of simmering in silence, address the issue. You might say, "I understand the project is urgent, but working late regularly is challenging for me. Can we discuss possible solutions?" This approach not only shows that you're committed to your work but also that you value your own time.

Balancing your personal and professional life is like walking a tightrope. Lean too much on one side, and you risk falling off. Setting and maintaining boundaries play a crucial role in this balancing act. They help you manage your time and energy so that you can give your best both at work and home. For instance, you might decide to dedicate Sundays to family, making it a gadget-free day, or choose to do yoga after work, signaling to your colleagues and yourself that the workday is officially over. These boundaries aren't just about keeping others at bay; they're about carving out time for what rejuvenates and refreshes you, ensuring you're not just productive but also happy and healthy.

In essence, establishing and maintaining boundaries is less about building walls and more about drawing lines that help you navigate through life effectively. It's about knowing when to say yes and how to say no, and feeling perfectly fine with both. By setting these boundaries, you not only protect your mental health and prevent burnout, but you also build stronger, more respectful relationships both professionally and personally. So, as you continue to navigate through your daily routines, remember that these boundaries aren't just optional; they are essential to your well-being and success. They are the silent sentinels that keep you focused, balanced, and at peace with your choices.

Emotional Regulation: Techniques to Maintain Your Cool

Let's face it, we've all been there—those moments when your blood boils, your chest tightens, and you're about a second away from saying or doing something you might regret. It's human. But here's the kicker: mastering your emotions isn't about stifling them; it's about understanding and managing them so they don't manage you. This is where emotional regulation swoops in, kind of like a superhero for your psyche, ensuring you keep your cool in situations that might otherwise make you hot under the collar.

Understanding Emotional Triggers

The first step in becoming a maestro of your emotions is to pinpoint what exactly plucks your heartstrings. Think of emotional triggers as those buttons that, when pushed, launch you into states of joy, anger, sadness, or fear. Recognizing these triggers is like mapping out a minefield—you need to know where the bombs are to avoid setting them off. Start by tracking your reactions for a few days. What ticked you off? What made you anxious? Was it a comment from a coworker, a specific type of workload, or maybe running late in the morning? Observations like these can reveal patterns and help you identify your personal emotional triggers. It's about becoming an observer of your own life, watching your emotional responses without judgment but with plenty of curiosity.

Strategies for Emotional Control

Now, onto the nitty-gritty of keeping your cool. One effective technique is cognitive re-framing, which basically means changing the way you look at a situation. It's like adjusting your mental lens. For instance, if you're stuck in traffic and fuming, re-frame the scenario: this is a perfect time to listen to your favorite podcast or unwind with some music. By shifting your perspective, the situation appears less aggravating and more like an unexpected break. Next up, there's deep breathing—simple yet profoundly effective. When you feel overwhelmed, take slow, deep breaths to lower your heart rate and invite calmness. It's like hitting the pause button, giving you a chance to reset. Then, there's the pause-and-plan approach, where you take a moment to stop and think before reacting. This pause can be the difference between a rash decision and a thoughtful response. Use this time to assess the situation and decide the best course of action that aligns with your goals and values.

Role of Emotional Intelligence in Regulation

Emotional intelligence (EI) is your ability to understand and manage not only your own emotions but also those of others. It plays a colossal role in emotional regulation. With high EI, you're better equipped to recognize your emotional triggers, understand what they mean, and decide how you'll react—all in real time. It's like having an internal emotional consultant that helps you navigate interactions smoothly. EI involves skills like empathy, which allows you to see things from another person's perspective, reducing conflicts and misunderstandings. It enhances your communication skills, making you more capable of expressing your feelings in a way that's constructive rather than destructive.

Practicing Emotional Regulation in Real Scenarios

Let's put this into practice with some role-play exercises that you can try out in your daily interactions. Imagine you're in a meeting and a colleague dismisses your idea. Instead of reacting defensively, employ your pause-and-plan technique. Take a deep breath, acknowledge your initial feelings, and then respond with, "I see you have a different perspective. Could you elaborate on your concerns so we can find a common ground?" This approach not only keeps the conversation productive but also positions you as a composed and considerate team player. Another scenario: you're criticized unfairly by a friend. Use cognitive re-framing to consider that perhaps they're lashing out due to stress and not because of something you've done. Address the situation with empathy, saying, "It seems like you're really upset. Want to talk about what's going on?" This opens up a dialogue for understanding rather than escalating the conflict.

By integrating these emotional regulation techniques into your life, you equip yourself with tools not just to survive emotional upheavals but to thrive amidst them. Whether you're navigating professional waters or personal relationships, understanding your emotional landscape and knowing how to navigate it effectively ensures that you remain in the driver's seat, no matter what the emotional climate.

The Power of Resilience: Bouncing Back from Failure

Resilience might sound like one of those buzzwords that self-help gurus throw around, but let's strip it down to its core: resilience is your ability to bounce back from setbacks, brush off the dust, and keep moving forward. It's not about never failing; it's about learning how to recover from those failures with your spirit and determination intact. In the real world, this means not crumbling under the pressure of a missed promotion, a failed project, or even personal misfortunes. It's about embracing the fact that while life can throw some serious curve-balls, you have the capacity to throw them right back.

Building this kind of resilience isn't something that happens overnight. It's more like building a muscle, gradually and through consistent effort. One way to strengthen this muscle is through exposure to minor stresses in a controlled way. Think of it as resilience training. Start with small challenges that you can overcome easily, like solving a complex puzzle, learning a new skill, or managing a small project. These challenges teach your brain and your psyche that yes, obstacles are surmountable. Over time, these small victories add up, boosting your confidence and preparing you for bigger hurdles.

Reflection is another crucial tool in building resilience. It's about taking a moment to look back at past experiences, not with regret or self-pity, but as valuable lessons. Reflecting on what went wrong, what went right, and how you handled various situations gives you insights into your own behavior and decision-making processes. Ask yourself, what could I have done differently? What did I learn from this experience? This isn't about dwelling on the past but about mining it for gems of wisdom that can guide future actions.

Now, let's talk about mindset shifts because the way you think about failure can dramatically affect your resilience. If you view failure as a catastrophic, end-of-the-world scenario, it's going to hit you hard. But if you see it as a natural part of the learning process, a step closer to success, it becomes less daunting. Cultivate a growth mindset, where challenges are opportunities for growth, and setbacks are just setups for comebacks. This shift in perspective can transform your approach to failure, turning it from something to be avoided at all costs into something that enhances your personal growth and learning.

To bring this concept to life, consider the stories of individuals who've demonstrated remarkable resilience in the face of adversity. Take J.K. Rowling, for example, who faced numerous rejections before finally publishing the Harry Potter series, which has since become a global phenomenon. Her story is a powerful reminder that rejection and failure are merely steps on the path to success. There's also the story of Thomas Edison, whose famous quote, "I have not failed. I've just found 10,000 ways that won't work," reflects his resilient approach towards inventing the light bulb. Edison's persistence through thousands of unsuccessful attempts is a testament to the resilience required to innovate and succeed.

These stories and strategies underline the essence of resilience: it's not about having an ironclad plan that never goes wrong, but about having an ironclad spirit that doesn't wane when the plan does go wrong. It's about standing up one more time than you've fallen and moving forward with the knowledge and strength gained from every fall. By continuously challenging yourself, reflecting on your experiences, and shifting your mindset towards growth and learning, you can build the kind of resilience that turns life's toughest challenges into your greatest achievements. So next time you face a setback, remember, it's not just an obstacle; it's an opportunity to fortify your resilience, refine your strategies, and rise stronger than before.

Using Technology to Enhance Mental Health

In this digital age, where technology is often blamed for adding to our stress, it's refreshing to know that the same innovations can also help us manage it. Think of technology not as a villain but as a tool—a Swiss Army knife for our mental health. Let's dive into how various digital platforms and devices can serve as allies in our quest for better mental well-being.

Let's start with digital tools designed specifically for mental health. Apps like Headspace and Calm have taken the world by storm, not just because they're user-friendly, but because they provide a pocket-sized sanctuary for mindfulness and meditation. These apps offer guided sessions that help reduce stress and anxiety, improve focus, and promote better sleep, all at the touch of a button. Then there's Moodfit, an app that tracks your mood and offers actionable insights to improve your mental health daily. It's like having a personal mental health coach in your pocket, one that reminds you to adjust your habits and mindset towards a healthier psychological state. These tools are particularly useful for those who might feel overwhelmed by traditional meditation practices or therapy sessions. They break down mental health care into manageable, everyday tasks, making the daunting task of "getting better" feel a lot more doable.

Moving on to virtual therapy and counseling, which has been a game-changer for many. Platforms like Talkspace and BetterHelp offer therapy services that connect you with licensed therapists via text, video, or voice calls. This means you can have your therapy session while curled up on your couch with a cup of tea, without the stress of traveling to an office. For those with hectic schedules, this flexibility can make the difference between getting help and letting stress accumulate. Virtual therapy also tends to be more affordable than traditional methods, making mental health care more accessible to those who might otherwise forego it due to cost. It's important, however, to ensure that the privacy and confidentiality of these services meet the standards you'd expect from an in-person session. Always check the credentials of the platform and the therapists to ensure you're receiving quality care.

Then, there's the world of wearable technology, which has made significant strides in stress management. Devices like the Fitbit or Apple Watch now come equipped with features that monitor your heart rate variability (HRV), a key indicator of stress levels. These devices can alert you when your stress levels are peaking, prompting you to take a break, breathe, or step away from whatever is causing the tension. Some even offer guided breathing exercises to help you calm down in real-time. Imagine you're in a heated meeting or dealing with a stressful project deadline. Your watch vibrates, you take a moment to follow a guided breathing exercise, and you return to the task at hand more centered and less stressed. It's a prime example of how technology can be a partner in managing your day-to-day stress.

On-line communities also play a crucial role in supporting mental health. Platforms like 7 Cups provide a space where you can anonymously connect with trained listeners and chat about anything that's weighing on your mind. It's not a replacement for professional therapy, but it offers a layer of immediate support that can be incredibly comforting. These communities can be particularly beneficial for those who feel isolated in their struggles, providing a sense of belonging and understanding that is crucial for mental well-being.

In conclusion, technology offers a unique set of tools that can be harnessed to enhance our mental health. From apps that train us in mindfulness to wearables that keep our stress in check, and platforms that offer professional and peer support, these digital solutions make it easier to take active steps towards a healthier mental state. As we continue to navigate a world where stress seems ever-present, these tools can be vital allies in maintaining our mental health and wellness.

So, as we wrap up this chapter, remember that technology, often seen as a source of stress, can actually be a powerful ally in managing it. With the right apps, devices, and platforms, we can take control of our mental well-being, making the journey towards a healthier mind not just possible, but also accessible. Now, let's turn the page and discover more tools and techniques that can help us cultivate a life of greater peace and fulfillment.

Part 2

Chapter 3: Enhancing Communication Skills

Let's face it, we could all use a little boost in our communication skills. It's like having a Swiss Army knife in your social toolkit—equally handy in boardrooms, at dinner parties, or when navigating the treacherous waters of family reunions. In this chapter, we're diving into the art of communication—not just blabbering more, but actually saying what you mean, understanding others better, and ensuring everyone walks away feeling heard and respected.

3.1 Active Listening: A Skill for Success

Focusing on the Speaker

Picture this: you're at a noisy cafe trying to have a conversation. You lean in, cup your ear, and focus intently on the person across from you. That's active listening—filtering out distractions and giving the speaker your undivided attention. It sounds simple, right? But in our world of pings, rings, and buzzes, focusing can feel like trying to read War and Peace at a rock concert. Active listening requires you to tune out distractions aggressively. This means silencing your phone, turning off the TV, or closing your laptop during conversations. And it's not just about ditching the tech; it involves tuning in with your body too. Nodding, maintaining eye contact, and leaning forward slightly are all non-verbal cues that say, "I'm here, and I'm listening." It's about creating a space where the speaker feels seen and heard, which can transform the quality of your interactions.

Clarifying and Confirming Understanding

Ever played the telephone game? Someone whispers a message, and by the time it reaches the last person, it's turned into something hilariously unrecognizable. While it's fun at parties, in real life, misunderstandings aren't usually a laughing matter. That's where clarifying comes in. It's about making sure the message hasn't morphed into something else by the time it reaches you. You can do this by paraphrasing what you've heard and asking for confirmation. Say something like, "So, what you're saying is..." or "Do I understand correctly that...?" This not only ensures you've got the facts straight but also shows the speaker that you're genuinely engaged. It's a simple tactic that can prevent a whole lot of confusion and conflict.

Empathetic Responses

Now, let's add a layer of empathy. Responding empathetically means acknowledging the speaker's feelings—validating them without necessarily agreeing with them. It's like saying, "I see where you're coming from," which can be incredibly validating. Imagine a friend tells you they're upset because they feel overlooked at work. An empathetic response might be, "That sounds really frustrating. Anyone would feel down in that situation." Notice, you're not offering solutions or dismissing their feelings as overreactions. You're simply acknowledging their emotional experience, which can make all the difference in how supported they feel.

Practical Exercises for Improvement

To turn this theory into practice, let's try some exercises. Start with a daily active listening challenge. Choose one conversation each day to practice your active listening skills fully. Focus solely on understanding the other person, using body language to show engagement, and clarifying their points. Another exercise could involve watching a movie or TV show and focusing on one character. Try to understand their motivations and emotions, then discuss your perceptions with a friend. These exercises aren't just about improving your listening skills—they're about enhancing your ability to connect with others on a deeper level, making your interactions more meaningful and satisfying.

By honing your active listening skills, you not only improve your ability to communicate effectively, but you also build stronger, more empathetic relationships. Whether in a professional setting, among friends, or at home, being a good listener is an invaluable skill that fosters deeper connections and understanding, turning everyday conversations into opportunities for growth and bonding. So, let's tune in—really tune in—and transform the way we interact with the world around us.

3.2 Assertiveness Training: Speak Up Without Stepping Over

Assertiveness is like the Goldilocks of communication styles—it's just right. It's not about being a wallflower nor about bulldozing over others. It's the sweet spot where you respect both your own boundaries and those of others. Understanding the difference between assertiveness and aggression is crucial. While aggression is about winning at all costs, often at someone else's expense, assertiveness is about expressing your thoughts and needs honestly while also considering others' rights and feelings. It's like being the captain of your ship without turning into a pirate.

Assertiveness starts with clear communication. It's about saying what you mean and meaning what you say, without being mean when you say it. Imagine you're in a team meeting and you disagree with a proposed strategy. An aggressive response might involve bluntly shooting down the idea, possibly demeaning the proposer. An assertive approach, however, would involve acknowledging the merits of the idea but expressing your concerns in a way that opens up a discussion rather than shutting it down. You might say, "I see the strengths in this strategy, but here are my concerns..." This not only keeps the communication lines open but also encourages a collaborative environment.

Role-playing can be an excellent way to practice assertiveness. It allows you to experiment with different responses in a controlled setting, which can be incredibly beneficial. For instance, you could role-play a scenario with a colleague or a friend where you practice expressing discomfort about a recurring issue, such as them being consistently late to meetings. By rehearsing, you can refine your words to sound confident and clear without being confrontational. Try switching roles too, so you can understand the situation from the other person's perspective. This practice can help you develop a more balanced approach and prepare you for real-life situations.

Building assertiveness is also an excellent way to boost your self-esteem and confidence. It's empowering to know that you can stand up for yourself and your ideas without stepping on others. This empowerment feeds back into your self-image, reinforcing that you are a person worthy of respect—both giving it and receiving it. As you become more comfortable being assertive, you'll find that it not only improves your professional relationships but also enhances your personal ones. You become better at setting and respecting boundaries, which is fundamental to healthy, balanced relationships.

The journey to becoming more assertive isn't about changing who you are; it's about refining how you express yourself. It's about ensuring your voice is heard and respected, not lost in the noise or, conversely, becoming the noise. As you practice, remember that each interaction is an opportunity to fine-tune your assertiveness skills.

With each conversation, you're not just speaking up more effectively; you're also building a stronger, more confident you, ready to tackle whatever comes your way with grace and conviction. So next time you find yourself in a situation where you need to assert yourself, take a deep breath, gather your thoughts, and communicate clearly and respectfully. The more you practice, the more natural it will become, and the stronger your relationships will be for it.

3.3 Non-Verbal Communication: Reading Beyond Words

Imagine walking into a room and, without anyone speaking a word, you can sense the mood swinging like a pendulum. That's the power of non-verbal communication—those silent signals that speak volumes. Whether it's a furrowed brow, a slumped posture, or a quick glance, our bodies are broadcasting stations, sending out messages that are just as impactful as any words we utter. Understanding the complex language of non-verbal cues can dramatically enhance your ability to communicate and interpret others' intentions and feelings.

Let's break down the components of non-verbal communication. Think of your body as an orchestra, where each part plays a critical role in delivering a performance—your message. Facial expressions are like the lead violin, conveying a wide range of emotions from joy to anger, surprise to sadness, without a single word. Gestures, whether a thumbs-up or a pointed finger, act like the booming drums, emphasizing points and expressing ideas dynamically. Your posture, on the other hand, is the bass, the undercurrent that gives off vibes of confidence or anxiety, openness or defensiveness. Then there's eye contact, the piano keys that can play soulful tunes of sincerity or jarring chords of insincerity. Each element works together to deliver a message that can align with or contradict what's being said verbally.

Now, interpreting these non-verbal cues accurately is a skill akin to a detective decoding clues at a crime scene. It requires keen observation and a bit of intuition. For instance, crossed arms might indicate that someone is defensive or uncomfortable, while prolonged eye contact could mean they're either genuinely engaged or aggressively challenging. Learning to read these cues involves paying attention not just to what is being shown, but also to the context. A smile at a funeral, for instance, isn't likely to indicate happiness but perhaps nervousness or discomfort. By tuning into these subtle signals, you can gain deeper insights into someone's true feelings and intentions, paving the way for more meaningful and effective interactions.

Aligning verbal messages with non-verbal cues is crucial for maintaining trust and credibility. Consider how confusing it would be if someone said they were happy while frowning or declared they were listening but kept glancing at their watch. This misalignment can lead to mistrust and miscommunication. To avoid this, strive to ensure that your body language reflects your words. If you're apologizing, for example, your face should show sincerity, and your posture humility. This congruence reassures the listener that you are genuine and trustworthy, strengthening your relationships and enhancing your communicative effectiveness.

Cultural differences significantly impact non-verbal communication, adding another layer of complexity. What is considered polite or affirmative in one culture can be seen as rude or negative in another. For instance, maintaining eye contact is viewed as a sign of confidence and honesty in many Western cultures, but it can be perceived as disrespectful or confrontational in some Asian cultures. Understanding these cultural nuances is vital, especially in our globalized world where interactions with diverse cultures are common. It helps prevent potential faux pas and fosters smoother, more respectful communication across different cultural contexts.

By mastering the art of non-verbal communication, you not only become more adept at reading others but also more skilled at presenting yourself effectively. It's about harmonizing the silent yet expressive language of your body with the spoken words, ensuring that you convey clear, consistent, and culturally sensitive messages. Whether you're negotiating a deal, consoling a friend, or presenting an idea, your ability to manage and interpret non-vertical cues can significantly influence the outcome of your interactions. So, the next time you're communicating, remember, it's not just about what you say but also how you say it—without saying anything at all.

3.4 Conflict Resolution Strategies for the Workplace

Navigating the choppy waters of workplace conflict without turning into a corporate pirate can seem like a tall order. It's like playing a high-stakes game of chess where every move matters and the board is made of eggshells. But, fear not! Identifying the roots of workplace conflicts and handling them with finesse can transform you from a novice sailor into the seasoned captain of a ship sailing smoothly on tranquil seas. So, let's unravel the mysteries of workplace conflict, from spotting the early signs to effectively mediating disputes, ensuring your workplace remains a bastion of harmony and productivity.

Identifying Sources of Conflict

Conflicts don't just pop out of thin air like some bad magic trick. They have triggers—common ones in the workplace include miscommunication, personality clashes, competition for resources, or differing values. It's like a detective game where you need to identify the usual suspects before you can address the problem. Start by becoming an astute observer. Notice changes in team dynamics: Are certain team meetings more heated than others? Do specific project discussions end with frustrated sighs or rolling eyes? These subtle clues can be telling. It's also helpful to have regular feedback sessions with your team, providing a safe space for issues to be aired before they fester into bigger problems. Think of it as doing regular maintenance on a car—it's much easier to change the oil regularly than to replace a seized engine down the road.

Effective Communication During Conflict

Once you've pinpointed the source of the conflict, the next step is tackling it head-on with clear, constructive communication. This isn't about putting band-aids on bullet holes; it's about addressing the root of the issue and finding a solution that works for everyone involved. When conflicts arise, encourage open dialogue by facilitating a meeting dedicated to resolving the issue. Approach the conversation with a mindset of understanding, not accusing. Use "I" statements to express how the situation affects you, rather than blaming the other person, which can escalate tensions. For example, say, "I feel overwhelmed when my ideas aren't considered in project discussions," instead of, "You never listen to my ideas!" This keeps the focus on resolving the issue rather than pointing fingers.

Mediation and Negotiation Skills

Sometimes, despite your best efforts, direct communication between parties isn't enough, and that's where your mediation skills come into play. Mediation is like being the referee in a game where both teams need to win. Start by ensuring all parties involved have the chance to express their perspectives without interruption. Your role here is to facilitate understanding, help clarify the real issues, and guide the discussion toward a mutually acceptable solution. Techniques like restating or summarizing what others have said can help ensure that everyone is on the same page. When it comes to negotiation, focus on finding the win-win. Encourage each side to make concessions that are valued by the other party. It's about compromise and creativity—sometimes the best solutions arise from thinking outside the box.

Preventing Future Conflicts

As the old saying goes, prevention is better than cure. Creating a workplace environment that minimizes potential conflicts is about nurturing a culture of open communication and respect. Establish clear communication protocols and ensure they are followed. Regular team-building activities can enhance mutual respect and understanding, reducing personal conflicts. Also, clear job descriptions and defined roles help prevent disputes over who is supposed to do what. Consider implementing conflict resolution training for your team. It equips everyone with the tools not just to manage but to prevent conflicts, fostering a more collaborative and productive workplace environment.

By becoming skilled in these conflict resolution strategies, you not only keep the peace; you also build a stronger, more cohesive team. Remember, conflict isn't necessarily the villain in your workplace saga—it can be an opportunity for growth and improvement if handled correctly. So, wear your mediator hat proudly, and steer your team through the storms of discord into the calm seas of collaborative success. With these strategies in your arsenal, you're well-equipped to handle whatever choppy waters might come your way.

3.5 Persuasion Techniques for Influential Leadership

Let's talk about persuasion—the art of getting others to see things your way without resorting to arm-twisting or, heaven forbid, boring PowerPoint presentations. It's about winning hearts and minds, and when done right, it can elevate your leadership from effective to downright transformative. Persuasion isn't about manipulation; it's about communication and understanding, combined with a dash of psychological savvy. So, buckle up as we decode the magic beans of persuasion that can grow your leadership skills to Jack-and-the-Beanstalk heights.

Principles of Persuasion

The principles of persuasion, a set of psychological triggers identified by Dr. Robert Cialdini, offer a blueprint for ethical influence. Let's start with reciprocity, the good old give-and-take formula. It's simple: when you do something nice for someone, they're likely to return the favor. In a leadership context, this could mean going the extra mile to support your team's professional development, which in turn, can foster loyalty and a strong work ethic. Next up, scarcity—people value what's in limited supply. Highlighting the unique opportunities that a project might offer can drive your team to engage more deeply. Authority is another key principle; showing that you have the chops—through expertise, experience, or demonstrated skill—can increase your persuasiveness. Consistency is about aligning your actions with your words; it builds trust and makes people more likely to follow your lead. Liking—yes, it helps if people actually like you. This can be achieved through shared interests, a congenial personality, or just being empathetic. Finally, there's consensus, showing that others have bought into an idea can encourage more people to follow suit. It's the "everyone's doing it" effect, but used judiciously and honestly.

Applying Persuasion in Leadership

Now, wielding these principles like a maestro leads an orchestra can transform the way you lead. It starts with understanding your team's values and needs. Engage with them, not just as employees, but as people with interests, fears, and ambitions. Use the principle of liking to connect on a personal level, which can make your persuasion efforts feel more genuine. Implement the principle of consistency by ensuring your actions mirror your commitments. If you promise an open-door policy, be there, ready to listen. Apply reciprocity by recognizing your team's efforts, perhaps with a shout-out during a meeting or a small reward. By showing appreciation, you're not just boosting morale but also encouraging a culture of mutual respect and motivation.

Case Studies of Persuasive Leaders

Consider the case of a tech CEO who led her company through a rough patch by meticulously applying these principles. She started by holding town hall meetings, addressing concerns with transparency (authority) and acknowledging the team's hard work (reciprocity). She outlined the unique position the company was in to revolutionize its sector (scarcity), consistently matched her actions with her words by following up on promises (consistency), and took time to engage with employees at all levels (liking). When the time came to introduce a controversial policy change, she demonstrated that similar initiatives had been successful in other organizations (consensus), which helped ease the transition. Her approach not only steered her company out of troubled waters but also boosted its innovation and employee satisfaction scores.

Developing a Persuasive Communication Style

Crafting a communication style that naturally incorporates these persuasion techniques starts with self-awareness and adaptability. Pay attention to how your message is being received and be ready to adjust your approach. Use stories and anecdotes to make your points more relateable and memorable, tapping into the liking principle. Be clear and concise, reducing your core message to easily digestible bits that don't require a decoder ring to understand. Practice active listening to understand your team's perspectives and needs better, which can inform how you apply the principles of persuasion more effectively. Remember, persuasion is a two-way street; it's as much about listening and adapting as it is about influencing.

By mastering these persuasion techniques, you can lead more effectively, foster a positive workplace, and drive your team towards shared goals with enthusiasm and commitment. It's about making every interaction count and every message clear, inspiring action and commitment through genuine connection and strategic communication. So, as you move forward, think of persuasion not just as a skill but as an essential element of your leadership style, one that respects, motivates, and elevates those around you.

3.6 Digital Communication: Navigating On-line Interactions

In our hyper-connected world, mastering the art of digital communication is akin to learning how to steer a ship through stormy seas. It's crucial, it's challenging, and yes, it's absolutely necessary. Whether it's email, social media, or instant messaging, each platform has its own set of unspoken rules and etiquette—an invisible handbook we're all supposed to somehow know. Let's decrypt some of these digital mysteries and ensure your on-line communication is as polished and professional as you are.

Etiquette and Professionalism in Digital Communication

Let's start with email—it's like the old soul of digital communication. The key here is clarity and brevity. Start your emails with a friendly greeting and get straight to the point. No one needs another novel in their inbox. And remember, tone is notoriously tricky to convey via text. What you meant as playful could be read as snarky. When in doubt, err on the side of formality. As for social media, think of it as the casual Friday of the digital world. It's less formal, but that doesn't mean anything goes. Always keep professionalism in the back of your mind, even when posting on more laid-back platforms like Twitter or Facebook. And instant messaging? It's the speedy, often chaotic younger sibling. It's tempting to treat it like a casual chat, but remember, those messages can be screen-shotted and saved, so keep it clean and professional, especially in work contexts.

Building Rapport On-line

Creating genuine connections on-line is like planting a garden through a letterbox—it's not easy, but it's not impossible either. It starts with being responsive. If someone comments on your LinkedIn post or sends an email, don't leave them hanging. A quick acknowledgment can go a long way in building trust and rapport. Next, personalize your communications. Include details in your messages that show you pay attention and care, like referencing a previous discussion or congratulating them on a recent achievement. It shows you see them as more than just another contact. Also, make an effort to engage regularly. Share relevant articles, congratulate contacts on their professional milestones, or simply check in. These interactions, though small, help build a network of genuine connections that can be invaluable both professionally and personally.

Managing Digital Communication Overload

Now, navigating the deluge of digital messages without capsizing can seem daunting. First, prioritize. Not all emails demand an immediate response. Learn to distinguish between what's urgent and what can wait. Use features like email flags or categorization tools to keep your inbox in check. Next, set boundaries. It's okay to close your email or messaging apps during deep-focus work sessions. You can even set an auto-responder to let people know when you'll be checking messages next. Lastly, consider a digital detox. Choose a day or even just a few hours a week where you consciously step away from digital communications. It helps reset your mind and reduces the risk of burnout, keeping you sharp and ready to tackle the high seas of digital dialogue.

Leveraging Digital Tools for Better Communication

In the vast ocean of digital tools, knowing which ones to have in your arsenal can make all the difference. CRM systems, for instance, can be a godsend for managing professional relationships, helping you keep track of interactions and important details about your contacts. Platforms like Zoom or Microsoft Teams have become cornerstones of virtual meetings, offering features that enhance collaboration, like screen sharing, virtual whiteboards, and real-time document collaboration. Then there's Slack, which streamlines team communication into channels, making it easier to track discussions and share files. Embrace these tools, and you'll find that managing your digital communications becomes more a matter of course than a cause for stress.

Navigating the intricacies of digital communication requires tact, awareness, and the right tools. By understanding the etiquette specific to each platform, actively building rapport, managing the influx of digital messages, and utilizing efficient communication tools, you strengthen your on-line presence and enhance your digital interactions. As we close this chapter on digital communication, remember that the goal is not just to keep up but to stand out. By mastering these digital nuances, you set yourself apart as a professional and a leader in the virtual world.

As we move forward, let's carry these communication skills into the broader context of personal development and leadership, remembering that every interaction, digital or otherwise, is a building block in the architecture of our professional lives. Let's continue to build wisely and communicate effectively.

Part 2

Chapter 4: Financial Management for Future Security

Welcome to the wild world of sorting your finances, where the excitement of managing your money smarter has all the thrills of a roller coaster—ups, downs, and a few loop-de-loops. But fear not, this ride won't leave you dizzy. Instead, it's going to arm you with the superpowers of budgeting, ensuring that you ride into the sunset of financial stability, rather than crashing into the scary land of 'Where Did All My Money Go?' Let's get into the nitty-gritty of budgeting basics, not just to keep your bank account happy, but to transform you into the savvy financial guru you were always meant to be.

4.1 Budgeting Basics: Managing Your Money Smarter

Understanding the Basics of Budgeting

Let's start with the ABCs of budgeting. Think of a budget as your financial road-map; it shows you where your money is coming from, tells you where it's going, and helps you make sure it's headed in the right direction. The core idea here is simple: know your income, control your expenses, and plan for both the short term and the long term. Why? Because without a budget, you're financially blindfolded.

You might make it across the street safely a few times, but eventually, you're going to bump into something unpleasant.

First up, tracking your income and expenses. This isn't about nickel-and-diming yourself for every coffee, but about understanding the larger flow of your financial life. How much money is coming in? Where is it coming from? On the flip side, where is it all going? Are your swanky dinners and gadget indulgences leaving a crater in your wallet? By laying out these figures, you can see the gaps between your income and spending, which is the first step in taking control of your cash flow.

Setting Up a Budget

Now, let's roll up our sleeves and set up your budget. This isn't about restricting your freedom; think of it more like setting up a game plan that helps you win at the money game. Start with the essentials—rent, utilities, food, and transport. These are non-negotiables, the must-haves. Next, allocate funds for your savings goals, whether it's the dream vacation, emergency fund, or the 'someday I'll retire' fund. Whatever is left can be your play money—for the movies, nights out, or whatever makes your heart sing.

Here's a pro tip: follow the 50/30/20 rule. It's a handy budgeting guideline where 50% of your income goes to necessities, 30% to wants, and 20% to savings. It's simple, clean, and surprisingly effective. Adjust the percentages to suit your reality, especially if you're in a high-cost living area or have specific financial goals. The key here is balance—ensuring that you cover your essentials, save for the future, and still have enough to enjoy life.

Tools and Apps for Budgeting

In this digital age, why not let technology do the heavy lifting? There's an arsenal of budgeting tools and apps out there that can simplify, and even automate, much of this process. Apps like Mint or

YNAB (You Need a Budget) link directly to your bank accounts and categorize your spending for you. They can help you set up budgets, track expenses, and even send alerts when you're about to go over budget. Then there's Tiller, a service that pulls all your financial information into customizable Google Sheets. It's like having a financial control center at your fingertips.

Adjusting Budgets Over Time

Your budget isn't set in stone. Life changes, and your budget should too. Got a raise? Maybe it's time to bump up your savings. Unexpected expenses? Time to tighten the belt for a bit. Review your budget monthly to adjust for life's ups and downs. This keeps you in control and prevents financial surprises from turning into disasters. Also, don't forget to include some wiggle room for those unforeseen expenses, because if life is anything, it's unpredictable.

Navigating through your financial landscape with a well-planned budget can turn the daunting world of money management into a well-marked treasure map. With the right tools, a bit of discipline, and a willingness to adjust as you go, you'll not only avoid financial pitfalls but also build a future where financial stability is your reality. So, let's keep this financial ship steady, chart a course through the budgeting seas, and sail towards that horizon of economic security and peace of mind.

4.2 Investing 102: An Introduction for Beginners

So, you've got your budget nailed down and a little extra cash on the side, and now you're peeking over the fence at the lush green pastures of investing. Let's demystify this financial frontier together, shall we? First off, investing isn't just for the monocle-wearing millionaires or those who speak in financial jargon. Nope, it's for anyone like you and me wanting our money to work a bit harder.

Let's start with the basics—stocks, bonds, mutual funds, and ETFs. Think of stocks as tiny slices of a company. Buy a stock, and voilá! You own a piece of that company. If the company does well, so do you; if it doesn't, well, your investment might not look so rosy. Bonds, on the other hand, are akin to loans that you give to companies or governments, and they pay you back with interest. Pretty straightforward, right? Now, mutual funds are like baskets of various investments—stocks, bonds, you name it—managed by financial pros. You put your money in, and they aim to grow it over time. ETFs or Exchange-Traded Funds are similar to mutual funds but with a twist—they trade on stock exchanges, just like stocks. This means you can buy and sell shares of ETFs throughout the trading day at market price.

Now, onto the roller-coaster part of investing—risk versus reward. Here's the deal: generally, the higher the potential return, the higher the risk. It's like the financial version of spicy food—the spicier you go, the more it might burn, but oh, the flavor could be worth it! Assessing your risk tolerance is key. It's about knowing how much volatility you can handle without losing sleep. Are you the type who's okay watching your investments rise and fall with the market's mood swings? Or does even a minor dip have you breaking out in a cold sweat? Understanding this about yourself is crucial before you dive into investing.

Starting small is the name of the game. You don't need to throw thousands into the stock market to begin. Many on-line platforms allow you to start investing with as little as $50. The trick is consistency. Think of investing like watering a plant—a little bit regularly can go a long way. Setting up automatic monthly contributions, even small ones, can help you build your investment over time without it feeling like a financial burden. It's about making investing a habit, much like any other good habit you've cultivated.

Lastly, arm yourself with knowledge. The world of investing is vast and can be complex, but thankfully, there's a wealth of resources out there. For starters, check out books like "The Intelligent Investor" by Benjamin Graham for a deep dive into investing principles, or "A Random Walk Down Wall Street" by Burton Malkiel to understand stock markets. Websites like Investopedia offer tons of articles and tutorials on every aspect of investing, and platforms like Morningstar provide in-depth research on stocks and mutual funds. If you're more of a listener, podcasts such as "The Motley Fool Money" can keep you updated on market trends and give you actionable investment tips in a way that's easy to digest.

Stepping into the world of investing can be as daunting as it is exciting, but with the right tools and a bit of knowledge, you can navigate this landscape with confidence. Remember, the goal of investing isn't just about making money; it's about making your money make money, securing your financial future one smart decision at a time. So, let's get those financial gears turning and start your investing adventure with a solid foundation and a keen eye on the horizon.

4.3 Building Multiple Income Streams

Let's talk about your financial landscape. Imagine it as a bustling city rather than a sleepy single-road town. That's what having multiple income streams can do for you—it turns a delicate single source of income into a thriving metropolis of opportunities. Diversifying your income is like having an insurance policy against the unpredictable ebbs and flows of the job market. It not only cushions you against sudden economic shocks but also opens up avenues for increased financial freedom and security. So, how does one go about building these various income streams? Well, it's part art, part science, and a whole lot of savvy maneuvering.

Firstly, let's explore the vast world of opportunities out there. Real estate investment is a classic choice. Whether it's buying a property to rent out or investing in real estate investment trusts (REITs), it's a path that can lead to solid passive income. Then there's the gig economy—ride-sharing, food delivery, freelance graphic design, writing, or even consulting. These gigs can be tailored to fit around your existing job and can significantly beef up your monthly income. E-commerce platforms offer another lucrative avenue. Starting an on-line store or flipping items on eBay could tap into your entrepreneurial spirit and turn a profit. And let's not forget about creating digital products—e-books, courses, or how-to guides. These can provide a steady income stream once they're up and running.

Balancing these ventures with your everyday life, however, is where the real challenge lies. It's like juggling flaming torches—it looks cool, but one wrong move can lead to a hot mess. The key here is prioritization and time management. Start small. Take on one extra income stream to see how it fits into your life before adding more. Use tools like Google Calendar or Trello to keep track of your commitments. Automate as much as possible. If you're investing in stocks or REITs, set up automatic monthly contributions. If you're running an e-commerce store, use software that handles some of the customer service or marketing for you. The goal is to make each venture as passive as possible, so it doesn't eat up all your free time.

Let's draw inspiration from some real-life case studies—people who've mastered the art of income diversification. Take Sarah, for example, a graphic designer by day, who started selling her designs on merchandise through an on-line platform. Her initial goal was just to make a bit of extra cash, but soon she was pulling in over a thousand dollars a month, passively! Then there's Mike, who bought a small condo in a tourist-friendly city. He started renting it out on Airbnb and managed to cover his mortgage and then some. These stories underscore the potential of side hustles and investments to not only provide extra income but also build lasting financial stability.

Navigating the complexities of multiple income streams requires a keen eye for opportunity, a good grasp of time management, and a bit of courage to step out of your financial comfort zone. But the payoff is more than worth it. It's about not putting all your financial eggs in one basket, but spreading them across several, ensuring that even if one breaks, you're not going to scramble to make ends meet. So, explore, evaluate, and experiment with different income streams. Each step you take down this road not only broadens your financial horizons but also brings you closer to achieving a level of financial security and independence that many only dream of.

4.4 Navigating Financial Crises: A Survival Guide

Imagine you're enjoying a peaceful boat ride. The sun is shining, the water is calm, and then out of nowhere, storm clouds gather, and the waves start rocking your boat. That's kind of what a financial crisis feels like—sudden, unsettling, and challenging to navigate. But don't worry, even if your financial boat feels a bit shaky, I've got some life jackets and paddles ready for you. Let's start by spotting those ominous clouds on the financial horizon before the storm hits.

Recognizing the early signs of a financial crisis can be as straightforward as noticing that your monthly expenses consistently outstrip your income. It's that simple and yet, that crucial. Or perhaps your credit card debt keeps growing, or you find yourself dipping into your savings just to cover regular bills. These are your financial warning signs, flashing red. Maybe it's the broader economic indicators you're watching—like sudden drops in the stock market, rising unemployment rates, or declining consumer spending. These can also hint at tougher times ahead. Keeping an eye on these signs isn't pessimistic; it's pragmatic. It's about being prepared, not scared.

Now, let's talk resilience—financial resilience. It's your safety net, your financial shock absorber. The cornerstone of this resilience? An emergency fund. This fund isn't the most exciting investment you'll ever make, but it is one of the smartest. Aim to sock away at least three to six months' worth of living expenses. It's like having a financial bunker, giving you a place to hunker down and ride out any economic turbulence without panicking. Diversifying your investments is your next line of defense. Don't put all your financial eggs in one basket. Spread them out—stocks, bonds, real estate, a mix of sectors and geographies. This diversification helps buffer your finances from taking a hit if one sector or market dips.

When the storm hits and you're in the thick of a financial setback, the first step is not to freeze or panic. Assess the damage. How deep are the cuts? What expenses can you trim without drastically affecting your quality of life? Maybe it's renegotiating your current mortgage or refinancing loans to lower interest rates. Perhaps it's cutting down on less critical subscriptions or discretionary spending. These actions are your financial triage, stopping the bleeding while you stabilize your situation. It's also the time to open communication lines with creditors or financial advisors. Be upfront about your financial challenges and explore options such as extended payment terms or reduced payments. Many creditors are more understanding when you approach them proactively and with a clear plan.

Here's something crucial—learning from the crisis. Every financial downturn carries valuable lessons. It's a harsh tutor, but the lessons on risk management, emergency preparedness, and the importance of savings are invaluable. Analyze what went wrong and why. Did you overestimate your income stability? Were your investments too risky? This reflection isn't about beating yourself up. It's about fortifying your financial strategy, so next time, and yes, there might be a next time, you're better fortified. It's about turning hindsight into foresight.

Navigating through financial crises requires a blend of vigilance, preparedness, and adaptability. By learning to read the signs early, building and maintaining your financial defenses, and thoughtfully navigating through crises, you equip yourself not just to survive but to emerge financially smarter and stronger. Remember, financial stability isn't about avoiding storms—it's about learning to sail in any weather, knowing you've prepared your boat, set your course, and are ready for whatever comes your way. So, keep your financial life jackets close, and let's keep sailing towards a secure financial future.

4.5 Retirement Planning: Starting Early to Secure Your Future

Let's get real about retirement. It's not just a distant phase where you suddenly switch from full-throttle to parked in the driveway. Retirement is like the dessert of your working life—it should be sweet, well-deserved, and thoroughly planned, so you're not left with just crumbs. Diving into retirement planning early isn't just a nice-to-do; it's a must-do if you want to keep your golden years golden. Think of it as planting a tree. Start early, and you'll enjoy ample shade and juicy fruits down the line. Ignore it, and well, you might just be left standing in the sun wondering where all the shade went.

Let's talk compound interest—it's the secret sauce of early retirement planning. Here's the scoop: the sooner you start saving, the more time your money has to grow through the magic of compounding. It's like rolling a snowball down a snowy hill; it starts small, but as it rolls, it grows bigger and faster. By starting early, you allow your savings to snowball, turning modest contributions now into a significant nest egg by the time you retire. This not only maximizes your investments but also slashes stress. Knowing you're financially prepared allows you to transition into retirement smoothly, without the panic of last-minute scrambling.

Now, onto the vehicles that can turbocharge your retirement savings. First up, the mighty 401(k). If your employer offers one, especially with a match, jump on that bandwagon fast. It's like getting free money, folks. Every dollar you contribute is taken from your paycheck before taxes, which means lower taxable income and less tax paid out of your current earnings. Plus, the money grows tax-deferred until you withdraw it in retirement, typically at a lower tax rate. Then there's the Individual Retirement Account (IRA), offering similar tax advantages with a bit more flexibility in investment choices. For those who anticipate a higher tax rate in retirement or simply want tax-free withdrawals later, consider the Roth IRA. You contribute after-tax dollars, but your withdrawals, including earnings, are tax-free in retirement. Each of these accounts has its nuances, benefits, and rules, so getting cozy with their details can help you maximize your retirement contributions effectively.

Calculating how much dough you'll need to retire comfortably is more art than science. Start by envisioning your ideal retirement lifestyle. Are you sipping margaritas on a beach, or are you happy gardening in your backyard? Each vision has a price tag. Factor in living expenses, healthcare costs, travel budgets, and, yes, even gifts for the grandkids. Don't forget inflation—it's the silent budget eater. A general rule of thumb is to aim for a nest egg that's 25 times your annual retirement expenses. Why? Because this can allow you to withdraw 4% of your savings each year without running dry. Tools like retirement calculators can crunch these numbers, taking into account your current age, income, savings rate, and other financial commitments. It's about painting a picture of your financial future that's as detailed and vivid as possible.

Adjusting your retirement plans as life evolves is crucial. Life throws curve balls—career changes, health issues, family needs—and your retirement plan needs to be flexible enough to catch them. Got a hefty raise? Maybe boost your retirement contributions. Facing unexpected medical expenses? It might be time to reassess your withdrawal plans or delay retirement to shore up finances. Regular check-ins with your financial advisor, or at least a hearty annual review of your retirement strategy, can keep you on track. It's about adapting, not just adhering to a set plan.

Navigating the road to retirement doesn't have to be a solo journey. With the right planning, tools, and mindset, you can pave a path that leads to a comfortable, secure retirement. Start early, invest wisely, and keep your plans flexible to accommodate the twists and turns of life. This proactive approach not only secures your future but also empowers you to enjoy the present, knowing that your later years are well taken care of. So, let's get planning and make sure that your retirement is everything you've hoped for and more.

4.6 Financial Negotiation Tactics: Getting What You Deserve

Let's dive into the art of financial negotiation, where every word you say, every number you crunch, and every silence you hold can swing fortunes in your favor. Whether it's securing a pay raise, hashing out loan terms, or navigating the complexities of purchase agreements, the ability to negotiate effectively can be a game-changer. It's less about the cold hard cash and more about the strategy behind getting the best deal for your buck while ensuring everyone walks away feeling like a winner.

Basics of Financial Negotiation

Negotiation in financial settings revolves around a few core principles that are as timeless as they are effective. First, know what you want but also be clear on what you can compromise on. This isn't just about getting a bigger slice of the pie but understanding the pie's total size and how it can be divided so all parties feel satisfied. Whether you're negotiating your salary or a car deal, your preparation should include understanding the market standards, the other party's potential constraints, and the unique value you bring to the table. It's about striking that delicate balance between demand and diplomacy.

Preparing for a Negotiation

Preparation is your secret weapon. Start with thorough research—know the benchmarks, such as the going salary for your role in your industry and region, or the average price of the car you want to buy. Knowledge is power, and in negotiation, it's your best ally. Next, define your walk-away point—the deal-breaker terms that are non-negotiable for you. This clarity will prevent you from getting swayed by fancy footwork or pressure tactics during the negotiation. Understanding the other party's needs can also give you leverage. What are they looking for in this deal? How can you align your proposals with their goals? This not only prepares you for the negotiation but also positions you as a solution provider, not just a beneficiary.

Effective Negotiation Strategies

When the negotiation begins, rapport-building is crucial. People are more likely to reach an agreement with someone they like and trust. Start on a positive note, be respectful, and listen actively. When it's time to talk numbers, being the first to throw out a figure can set the anchor for the negotiation, known as the anchoring bias. Make your offer reasonable but always on the higher side of your expectations—give yourself room to come down. And here's where silence is golden. After making your offer, pause. Let it sink in. Resist the urge to fill the silence with justifications or modifications to your offer. This silence can put pressure on the other party to respond or counteroffer, often leading them to reveal more about their flexibility or constraints than they intended.

Practicing Ethical Negotiation

Maintaining integrity and ethics in your negotiations ensures that deals are not only profitable but sustainable. High-pressure tactics or misleading information might get you a win today but can damage long-term relationships and reputations. Instead, strive for honest and transparent negotiations. Make sure that the terms are clear and that commitments are realistic. This builds trust and respect, laying the groundwork for future negotiations and ongoing business relationships. Remember, a successful negotiation is one where all parties feel like they've won.

Navigating the nuances of financial negotiation with these strategies can transform it from a dread-filled confrontation to an exciting opportunity to showcase your value and meet your financial goals. Whether you're discussing salaries, loans, or contracts, a well-negotiated deal not only brings immediate financial benefits but also sets a tone of professionalism and respect that can define your financial interactions for years to come.

As we wrap up this exploration of financial negotiation tactics, remember that the key to effective negotiation lies in preparation, clear communication, strategic silence, and a commitment to ethical dealings. These elements form the cornerstone of not just successful negotiations but also long-lasting professional relationships and financial stability. As you move forward, carry these tactics into all your financial dealings, ensuring that you not only get what you deserve but also build a reputation as a fair and savvy negotiator. Now, let's turn the page and discover more strategies that will further enhance your financial prowess and preparedness in the next chapter.

Part 2

Chapter 5: Productivity and Time Management

Imagine if you could command time—stretch it, shrink it, bend it to your will. Sounds like a superhero power, right? Well, buckle up, because I'm about to hand you the cape. In this chapter, we won't be fiddling with the space-time continuum, but we will dive into the next best thing: mastering productivity and time management. It's about making time your ally, not your enemy, and ensuring each tick of the clock pushes you closer to your personal and professional zeniths.

5.1 Prioritization Techniques That Work

Understanding Prioritization Frameworks

Navigating the bustling city of your daily tasks requires a reliable GPS—Good Prioritization Strategy. Let's talk about two killer strategies: the Eisenhower Box and the ABCDE method. Picture Eisenhower's Box as a simple four-quadrant chart that helps you decide on and prioritize tasks by urgency and importance, sorting out less urgent and important tasks which you should either delegate or not do at all. Then there's the ABCDE method, an extended family of the classic to-do list. Here, you label each task with a letter: 'A' for must-do critical tasks, 'B' for should-do important tasks, 'C' for nice-to-do tasks, 'D' for delegate, and 'E' for eliminate. It's like giving your tasks a grade based on how vital they are to your success each day.

These frameworks aren't just fancy acronyms; they're about making smart choices. Every day, you're bombarded with tasks that demand attention, but not all of them deserve your time. Picture this: Your boss wants a presentation by tomorrow, your colleague needs help with a project, your email inbox is overflowing, and your phone keeps buzzing with social media notifications. The Eisenhower Box helps you quickly discern between what needs your immediate attention and what can wait. Meanwhile, the ABCDE method gives you a hierarchy of focus, ensuring you're not putting energy into low-impact activities that drain your time and attention away from where they're really needed.

Aligning Priorities with Goals

The secret sauce to effective prioritization? Alignment with your long-term goals. If your goal is to get promoted, prioritize tasks that enhance your skills and visibility within your company. Each task on your list should be a stepping stone towards your larger goals. Think of it as setting up dominoes; each task nudges you closer to toppling over your big, audacious goals.

But how do you make this practical? Start with your ultimate objectives, and work backward to the daily stuff. If your goal is to write a book, your daily tasks should include dedicated writing time, research, and so forth. This ensures that every check on your to-do list is not just a task completed but a mini-victory towards achieving your dreams.

Handling Competing Priorities

Now, what about those days when everything seems urgent? Balancing competing priorities is like being a DJ at a party where everyone wants their song played next. You've got to mix and match, ensuring the dance floor stays packed. The key is flexibility coupled with a firm understanding of your goals. Some tasks might seem urgent, but are they important? This is where quick, decisive thinking comes in. You need to assess the impact of each task, how they align with your goals, and the consequences of delaying them.

One effective technique is the 'Rapid Decision Method'—set a timer for 1 minute, list all tasks at hand, and decide quickly which task will have the greatest impact or is the most urgent. This prevents decision fatigue and keeps you moving forward even in high-pressure situations.

Prioritization Tools

In our digital age, several tools can help keep your priorities clear and your progress on track. Digital tools like Trello or Asana allow you to organize tasks into boards and lists, making it easy to see what needs immediate attention and what can wait. These tools are like having a personal assistant who's always reminding you of what's up next. On the analog side, never underestimate the power of a well-organized planner or simple sticky notes on your workspace. They provide a tangible way to see your day at a glance and adjust as necessary.

Prioritization isn't just about getting things done; it's about getting the right things done. It's about making intentional choices with how you spend your hours, ensuring that each day moves you closer to your personal and professional peaks. By mastering these prioritization techniques, you transform your to-do list from a source of stress to a well-oiled road-map guiding you to success. Let's keep this momentum going and turn your newfound prioritization prowess into a catalyst for unprecedented productivity and time mastery.

5.2 The Art of Delegation: Doing Less to Do More

Delegation is not just a fancy business term for dumping your unwanted tasks on others; it's an art form that, when done right, can significantly amplify your productivity and enhance your team's capability. Think of it as being the conductor of an orchestra. You wouldn't play every instrument yourself, right? Instead, you guide and direct each musician to contribute their best, resulting in beautiful harmony. To master the art of delegation, you first need to understand which tasks to pass along and how to do so effectively.

Identifying which tasks to delegate is like sorting through your closet. You're looking for items that don't fit you anymore but could be a treasure for someone else. Start by assessing the complexity of the tasks at hand—can they be broken down into simpler steps? If yes, these are prime candidates for delegation. Next, consider the expertise required. If a task aligns better with the skill set of a colleague, delegating it could lead to better results and a learning opportunity for them. Then there's your personal learning curve. If a task is not within your zone of genius and would require an disproportionate amount of your time to master, it's probably wise to hand it off to someone who can handle it more efficiently.

Choosing the right person for each task is like casting for a movie. You want stars in roles that make them shine. This means looking beyond just skills; you need to consider the track records—how have they handled similar tasks before? Also, assess their current workload. Overloading a high-performer can lead to burnout and diminish the quality of their work. It's about striking that balance between their capability and capacity. Sometimes, the right choice might be to train someone less experienced. This investment can pay off immensely, fostering growth and increasing your team's overall skill level.

Now, let's talk about setting the stage right. Providing clear, concise instructions and expected outcomes is crucial. It's like giving a painter a vision of the finished artwork along with the colors and brushes they'll need. Be specific about what success looks like for each task and the timeline for completion. This clarity not only sets expectations but also empowers the delegate to deliver exactly what's needed. It eliminates guesswork and minimizes the back-and-forth that can often slow down progress. Remember, ambiguity is the enemy of effective delegation.

Constructive Feedback and Adjustments

Feedback is the breakfast of champions, and in the context of delegation, it's what ensures continuous improvement and success. After a task is completed, take the time to review the outcomes together. Highlight what went well and discuss areas for improvement. This feedback should be constructive, focusing on the process and outcomes, not on the person. It's not about pointing fingers but about learning and growing together. Moreover, be open to receiving feedback on your instructions and support throughout the process. Maybe your guidance was a bit too vague, or perhaps you didn't provide the resources they needed. This two-way feedback loop can strengthen your approach to delegation, making each iteration more effective than the last.

Mastering the art of delegation not only enhances your productivity but also motivates your team by trusting them with important tasks, leading to a more engaged and capable workforce. It's about recognizing that you don't have to do it all alone—by delegating effectively, you multiply your effectiveness and foster a spirit of teamwork and growth. So, start passing those batons; it's time to conduct your symphony!

5.3 Overcoming the Tyranny of the Urgent

Ever felt like your day is a series of fire-fighting episodes, jumping from one urgent task to another until the sun sets? We've all been there, where the urgent constantly nips at the heels of the important. Understanding the difference between what's urgent and what's important can be a total game-changer in how you manage your time and stress. Urgent tasks scream for immediate attention—they're the pop-ups of real life. Important tasks, however, are more like your system updates; they might not demand immediate attention but are crucial for long-term success. For instance, responding to an avalanche of emails might feel urgent, but strategizing for an upcoming project is important. The trick is not letting the urgent tasks overshadow the important ones which contribute significantly to your overarching goals.

Managing urgent tasks without letting them throw you off your game requires a blend of strategy and steel nerves. Start by creating a 'triage system' for your tasks. When faced with a new "urgent" task, ask yourself: Does this need to be done now, or can it wait? Is there someone else who can handle this? What are the consequences if I delay this task? This quick assessment can help you prioritize effectively and keep your focus on tasks that align with your goals. Another technique is to allocate specific times of your day to handle these urgent tasks. Think of it as containment—like setting boundaries for a pet that loves to run wild. Schedule an hour or two where you tackle these tasks head-on, and then return to your important tasks without guilt or stress.

Proactive planning is your best defense against the tyranny of the urgent. It's about foreseeing potential fires and dousing them before they flare up. This might mean setting clear deadlines for projects way before they're due or breaking down larger projects into manageable tasks and starting on them early. It's also about being clear on your capacities and setting realistic expectations with colleagues and clients. This not only minimizes last-minute rushes but also sets a professional tone of reliability and foresight. Implementing preventive strategies like these reduces the chaos of urgent tasks and allows you to operate from a place of control and foresight.

Stress management in these high-pressure situations is crucial. When urgent tasks do arise, and let's be honest, they always will, having a toolkit to manage stress can keep you from burning out. Techniques such as deep breathing exercises or a quick walk around the block can lower your stress hormones and give you a clearer head to tackle the urgency with precision. Also, maintain a regular practice of mindfulness or meditation; these are not just buzzwords but powerful tools that enhance your resilience against stress. They teach you to maintain calm and clarity under pressure, ensuring that you handle urgent tasks with a composed demeanor.

Employing these strategies to differentiate and manage urgent tasks, while keeping a keen eye on the important, reshapes your relationship with time and tasks. It ensures that you're not just reacting to what the day throws at you but actively orchestrating your day to align with your long-term visions and goals. By mastering the art of triaging, planning proactively, and managing stress, you turn what was once a tyranny of the urgent into a manageable aspect of your daily routine, allowing you to focus on not just the loud and immediate but also on the significant and transformative.

5.4 Tools and Apps for Time Management Mastery

Imagine your day as a jigsaw puzzle. Some pieces fit perfectly, while others seem to come from another box entirely. This is where time management tools step in, serving as the puzzle box lid, offering you the big picture to help guide your daily decisions and actions. Let's explore the digital landscape of time management tools, from calendar apps that keep your appointments in check, to task managers that remind you of your to-do list, and project tracking systems that keep your team on track. These tools are not just about keeping busy, they're about staying smartly busy, ensuring every piece of your daily puzzle fits just right.

First up, calendar apps like Google Calendar or Outlook are the unsung heroes in the quest for time mastery. They do more than just remind you of meetings; they are the scaffolds around which you can structure your day. With features that allow you to block out focus time, set reminders for deadlines, and schedule meetings without the back-and-forth emails, they are indispensable. But here's where the magic happens: customization. Not everyone's day looks the same, and these tools adapt to that. Color-coding different types of activities, setting up customizable alerts, and integrating with other apps like Trello or Asana can transform your basic calendar into a powerful, personalized time management hub.

Speaking of Trello and Asana, let's talk task managers and project tracking systems. These tools take the nitty-gritty details of your various projects and organize them into digestible, actionable panels or lists. Whether you're planning a marketing campaign, launching a new product, or just trying to keep your daily tasks in order, these platforms help you keep an eye on the big picture without losing sight of the small steps. Customization here is key. You can set up workflows that match your team's process, use labels to indicate priorities, or automate routine tasks to save time. By tailoring these tools to fit your specific needs, you turn a generic platform into a command center that mirrors the unique rhythms and requirements of your work life.

Integration of these tools creates a cohesive system that can significantly amplify your productivity. Imagine this: your project management tool is linked to your calendar. When you update a deadline in Asana, it automatically blocks out preparation time in your Google Calendar. At the same time, a reminder pops up on your phone, thanks to an integration with a mobile to-do list app like Todoist. This interconnectedness ensures that nothing falls through the cracks and that your tools are working together, not in isolation. It's about creating a seamless workflow where each tool completes the others, making your day smoother and your tasks more manageable.

Regular evaluation of the effectiveness of these tools is crucial. It's not a 'set it and forget it' deal. You need to check in periodically to ensure they are still serving your evolving needs. Are you spending too much time managing the tools rather than doing actual work? Are there features you never use, or worse, features you need but don't have? Most apps provide analytics that can help you understand how you interact with the tool and where bottlenecks might occur. Use this data to make informed decisions about which tools stay, which can be tweaked, and which should be replaced. Remember, the goal is to enhance your productivity, not to add another layer of complexity to your workday.

In mastering these digital tools, you transform them from mere applications on your screen into allies in your quest for productivity and time management. By customizing them to fit your personal style and professional demands, integrating them to create a streamlined workflow, and regularly evaluating their impact, you ensure that your time management tools are as dynamic and adaptable as you are. With these digital solutions in your arsenal, you're well-equipped to tackle your tasks with precision, keep your projects on track, and maybe, just maybe, find a little extra time to relax.

5.5 Creating a Distraction-Free Work Environment

Imagine your workspace as your personal command center. It's where you make big decisions, create, plan, and execute. Now, what if your command center is constantly under siege? Not by aliens or superheroes, but by a relentless barrage of distractions that chip away at your productivity like a woodpecker on a tree. Whether it's the ping of a new email, the buzz of your phone, or just the clutter on your desk, distractions are the arch-nemeses of focus. Let's gear up to defend your space and turn it into a fortress of concentration and effectiveness.

Identifying Common Distractions

Step one in our battle against distractions is identifying the enemy. Start by observing your typical day. What pulls your attention away most often? For many of us, it's our digital devices. Emails, instant messages, social media notifications—they demand our attention with the urgency of a five-alarm fire. Then there are the interruptions from colleagues or family members, which, while often well-meaning, can scatter our thoughts and derail our focus. And let's not overlook personal habits—like that compulsive checking of your phone or the 'quick' breaks that mysteriously turn into half-hour detours. Recognizing these distractions is like mapping the battlefield. Once you know where the attacks are coming from, you can fortify your defenses accordingly.

Physical Workspace Adjustments

Now, let's talk about fortifying your physical space. Think of it as setting up camp in a way that minimizes threats. Start with your desk. A cluttered desk can be a minefield of distractions. Each unsorted pile or unnecessary gadget is a visual cue that can pull your focus. Take a minimalist approach—keep only what you need for your daily tasks within arms' reach. Everything else can be stored away or left out of sight. Next, consider your ergonomics. Adjust your chair, desk, and computer monitor so that they promote good posture. Discomfort is a distraction that's easy to overlook but simple to fix. Managing noise is another crucial strategy. If you're in a noisy environment, noise-canceling headphones can be a game-changer. Or, if feasible, set up a quieter, dedicated workspace away from high-traffic areas. The goal here is to create a space that enhances focus, not fractures it.

Digital Discipline

In the digital realm, discipline is your main tactic. Start with notification management. Turn off non-essential notifications on your computer and smartphone. For the essentials, schedule specific times to check them—maybe once every hour or at natural breaks in your work. This prevents you from being in a constant reactive mode and helps maintain a proactive stance towards your tasks. Email is a notorious time-sink. Instead of keeping your email open all day, try checking it at set intervals—perhaps mid-morning, after lunch, and late afternoon. This limits the interruption caused by the constant influx of messages and keeps your email from dictating the pace of your day. For those websites that suck you in and spit you out an hour later wondering where the time went, consider website blockers like Freedom or Cold Turkey. These tools can help keep your on-line browsing focused during work hours.

Creating Routines for Focus

Finally, establishing routines that enhance focus can shield you from both external and internal distractions. The Pomodoro Technique is a popular method where you work for 25 minutes, then break for five, repeating this cycle throughout the day. This not only structures your work time but also integrates short breaks to clear your mind, keeping your mental energy balanced throughout the day. Another effective routine is planning your day with focus blocks—designated periods where you do nothing but dive deep into your tasks. During these blocks, make yourself unavailable as much as possible—turn off your phone, close your door, and dive into the deep work. These routines aren't just about working harder; they're about working smarter, creating pockets of high efficiency that can dramatically boost your productivity.

By transforming your workspace into a distraction-free zone, you're not just setting up a place to work; you're engineering an environment that enhances focus, boosts productivity, and ensures that you're operating at your best. It's about taking control of your space and your time, turning your daily work sessions into periods of meaningful and effective productivity. So, let's keep this momentum going and continue to optimize our work habits and environments to achieve the maximum impact in everything we do.

5.6 Time Audit: Analyzing How You Spend Your Days

Ever felt like your days are slipping through your fingers like sand? You're not alone. Many of us wonder where our time goes, especially on those whirlwind days when our to-do list seems untouched at sunset. That's where a time audit can shine a spotlight on your daily activities, revealing not just where your time goes, but also how you can reclaim it and perhaps even find time to spare. A time audit is like having a CCTV system on your daily routines; it provides undeniable evidence of your habits, both good and bad.

First up, let's break down what a time audit can unwrap for you. By tracking every activity, from the moment you sip your morning coffee to when you turn off your bedside lamp, you can pinpoint exactly where your time leaks are. Perhaps you're spending a surprising amount of time on social media, or maybe those 'quick' chats with colleagues are eating up more of your day than you realized. A time audit lays it all out in black and white, showing you not just where you might be wasting time, but also where you're being most productive. It's about identifying both the thieves and the golden geese of your time. The beauty of this revelation is that it empowers you to make informed decisions about how to better structure your day. It's like being given a map of an unknown city; suddenly, navigating becomes a lot easier.

Conducting a time audit isn't rocket science, but it does require commitment. Here's how you can do it effectively:

- Choose Your Method: You can go old-school with a pen and notepad, jotting down activities as you go, or digital with apps like Toggl or RescueTime, which track your activities automatically.

- Set a Timeframe: A week is ideal because it provides a comprehensive view of your typical patterns, including both weekdays and weekends.

- Record Everything: And I mean everything. Every phone call, every trip to the coffee machine, every minute spent browsing on-line. No detail is too small.

- Categorize: Group activities into categories like work, leisure, chores, etc. This will make the analysis easier.

Once your audit week is up, it's time to dive into the data. Analyzing the results from your time audit can be eye-opening. Lay out your findings and look for patterns. How much time are you spending on productive activities versus distractions? Are there times of day when you're more focused? This analysis can reveal inefficiencies and habits that, once adjusted, can significantly boost your productivity. For instance, if you discover you're most alert and efficient in the mornings, you might decide to tackle your most challenging tasks during this time and save routine tasks for the afternoon slump.

The final step is all about action—implementing changes based on your findings. This is where the rubber meets the road. If you've discovered that you spend a hefty chunk of your morning on emails, perhaps you'll decide to limit email checks to specific times. Or, if social media emerges as a major time sink, you might use app blockers during work hours to keep you focused. The key here is to create actionable steps that are realistic and measurable. Small tweaks can lead to significant gains in how you manage your time and productivity.

By conducting a time audit, you not only become more aware of how you spend your time but also equip yourself with the knowledge to improve your time management strategies. This process isn't about restricting your freedom but enhancing it, giving you more control over your day and ultimately, over your life's trajectory. So, as we wrap up this chapter, remember that understanding and managing your time effectively is foundational to living a productive and fulfilling life. Let's carry forward these insights and strategies as we continue to explore more avenues for personal and professional growth in the upcoming chapters.

Part 2

Chapter 6: Personal Development and Self-Care

Ever felt like your brain's in a rut? Like you're just going through the motions, and the zest for learning and exploring seems like a distant memory from your more sprightly days? Well, buckle up, my friend, because it's time to shake off that dust. We're about to reignite that spark of curiosity and transform it into a roaring fire of continual growth and learning. It's not just about adding new titles to your resume or brushing up on the latest industry buzzwords— it's about cultivating a mindset that thrives on challenges and views every experience as a stepping stone to a better you.

6.1 The Lifelong Learning Mindset: Strategies for Continuous Growth

Embracing Curiosity and Open-Mindedness

First off, let's talk about maintaining a curious mindset. Remember when you were a kid and every little thing seemed fascinating? Somehow, as we stride deeper into adulthood, that innate curiosity often dims under the weight of responsibilities and routines. But here's the secret sauce to personal growth: reigniting that childlike wonder. Curiosity is the engine of lifelong learning. It pushes you to ask questions, seek new experiences, and open doors to opportunities that wouldn't appear otherwise. It's about looking at familiar situations through a fresh lens—asking 'why' and 'what if' more often. This mindset doesn't just make life more interesting; it also keeps you mentally sharp and emotionally engaged.

To foster this openness, start by stepping out of your comfort zone regularly. Try a new hobby, travel to unfamiliar places, or simply switch up your daily routines. Each new experience is a neuron waiting to be woken up in your brain, expanding your perspective and challenging your assumptions. And hey, you might just find a new passion in the process.

Setting Learning Goals

Now, onto setting effective learning goals. It's easy to say you want to 'learn more' but what does that actually look like? This is where SMART criteria—Specific, Measurable, Achievable, Relevant, Time-bound—come into play. Suppose you're aiming to boost your skills in digital marketing. A SMART goal would be, "I will complete an on-line course on social media marketing by the end of Q3, dedicating two hours each week to watch lectures and complete assignments." This method not only sets a clear target but also outlines a manageable path to get there.

Setting learning goals aligned with both your career aspirations and personal interests keeps the motivation engine running. Whether you're looking to climb the career ladder or just expand your horizons, aligning your goals with your passions ensures that the learning process is enjoyable and deeply rewarding.

Leveraging Resources for Learning

The resources available today for learning are vast and varied—on-line courses, workshops, podcasts, books, the list goes on. Platforms like Coursera, LinkedIn Learning, and Khan Academy offer courses on everything from quantum physics to basket weaving. Podcasts can turn your commute into a mini-classroom, offering insights from industry leaders and thinkers just a play button away. And let's not forget books—the old faithfuls of knowledge. Whether you prefer digital or the good old paper kind, books remain invaluable treasures of learning.

The key to effectively utilizing these resources is to choose formats that fit your lifestyle and learning preference. Love visuals? On-line video tutorials might be your best bet. Always on the go? Audiobooks and podcasts can be your learning companions during your daily travels.

Reflecting and Journaling for Growth

Lastly, reflection is the mirror through which the value of all learning is truly seen. Maintaining a journal allows you to track your learning progress, reflect on new insights, and consolidate your thoughts. It's not just about jotting down what you learned, but also how you can apply it, and what changes you've noticed in your thinking or skills. This practice not only reinforces learning but also encourages a habit of critical thinking and self-evaluation.

Consider this: at the end of each week, take a moment to write down key learnings, how they apply to your life, and any new questions that have surfaced. This not only serves as a great way to de-clutter your mind but also creates a personal growth log that's incredibly satisfying to look back on.

By embracing curiosity, setting targeted learning goals, leveraging a plethora of resources, and reflecting through journaling, you transform yourself into a perpetual learner—adaptable, informed, and always evolving. So, let's keep this learning train chugging, shall we? Onwards to the next chapter of your development!

6.2 Physical Health and Its Impact on Personal Efficiency

Ah, physical health—often we treat it like the WIFI signal in a coffee shop; we only notice it when it starts to falter. But let's flip the script and talk about how staying physically fit isn't just about avoiding the doctor or fitting into those jeans from your college days. It's fundamentally linked to how effectively you can think, work, and just enjoy life. Good physical health acts like a turbocharger for your energy levels and mental clarity, making it easier to power through your to-do list and still have fuel left for fun.

Think about the last time you had to work through a cold. It was miserable, right? Your body felt like it was filled with lead, and your brain was wrapped in cotton wool. Now imagine feeling close to that every day because you're not taking care of your health. Not exactly a recipe for productivity. On the flip side, when you're feeling good physically, you're also sharper mentally. Research points to a clear link between regular physical activity and improved brain function, including quicker learning, better memory, and clearer thinking. This means that maintaining your health is not just about your body but about setting up your brain for success too.

Now, I get it, we're all busy, and sometimes it feels like there's just no time for a check-up or a treadmill session. But integrating health checks into your routine is critical. Think of it as regular maintenance for your most valuable asset—you! Regular health screenings catch potential issues early, saving you from more severe complications down the line. Simple things like monitoring your blood pressure, cholesterol levels, and other vitals can give you a clear picture of where you stand health-wise and what adjustments might be needed. It's like doing a systems check on a high-performance sports car; you want everything running smoothly to enjoy the ride and avoid breakdowns.

Let's talk exercise. It's not just about pumping iron or running marathons; it's about finding activities that fit into your life and make you feel good. Physical exercise boosts your brain's dopamine, norepinephrine, and serotonin levels—all of which affect focus and attention. In simpler terms, getting your body moving can sharpen your mind and lighten your mood, kind of like clearing the cobwebs from your attic. And the best part? There are many ways to get these benefits. From yoga, which keeps your joints happy and your mind calm, to something like kickboxing, which lets you punch away the day's stress. Even brisk walking can kickstart these chemical processes in your brain. The key is consistency and enjoyment. If you love what you do, it won't feel like a chore, and you'll stick to it.

Balancing work and health is akin to being a DJ at a great party; you need to keep the beats rolling without burning out your speakers. Integrating physical activity into a hectic schedule can be as simple as adopting the concept of 'exercise snacking'. No, it's not about munching on granola bars mid-jog; it's about short bursts of activity spread throughout the day. Take a quick walk around the block, do some stair climbing between meetings, or even some desk-based stretches. Another smart strategy is active commuting; if you can walk or bike to work, you're killing two birds with one stone, getting to work and getting in shape. It's about making your health regimen fit your life, not the other way around.

So, as we continue to explore the avenues of personal development and self-care, remember that your physical health is not just a foundation but a launching pad. It enhances your energy, sharpens your mind, and yes, it can even make those endless meetings a bit more bearable. Let's keep moving, not just towards our goals but towards a healthier, more vibrant life where we can enjoy every step of the way.

6.3 The Science of Sleep: Resting Towards Success

Let's talk about something we all love but often skimp on: sleep. If you've ever pulled an all-nighter or had a baby, you know exactly what sleep deprivation does to your mind and body. It's like trying to drive a car without fuel; you're not going to get very far. Yet, in our busy lives, sleep is often the first thing we sacrifice at the altar of productivity. But here's the twist: cutting back on sleep doesn't make us more productive. Quite the opposite, it's like stepping over dollars to pick up pennies. Understanding the science of sleep, its cycles, and its profound impact on our overall well-being can be a game-changer for how you approach your nightly snooze.

First up, let's dive into sleep cycles. Sleep isn't just a block of time where your body shuts off. Oh no, it's an intricate dance of phases, each crucial for different aspects of health and well-being. Generally, sleep is divided into non-REM and REM (Rapid Eye Movement) stages, cycling through these phases approximately every 90 minutes. Non-REM sleep kicks off the cycle and is divided into three stages: from the light nod-off phase to the deep, restorative stages where your body repairs muscle, consolidates memories, and releases growth hormones. Then comes the star of the show: REM sleep. This is where your brain gets busy processing emotions, forming memories, and basically doing a big nightly clean-up of your neural pathways. Skimp on these cycles, and both your body and brain will let you know, loud and clear.

Now, how can we enhance the quality of this precious sleep? It starts with what sleep experts call 'sleep hygiene'—no, it's not about brushing your teeth, though that's important too. It's about crafting a pre-sleep routine and environment that ushers you into dreamland smoothly. Dim the lights an hour before bed—yes, this means stepping away from your beloved screens—to help cue your brain that it's time to wind down. Keep your bedroom cool, quiet, and dark, like a cave (albeit a comfortable one). Invest in a good mattress and pillows because comfort isn't just luxurious; it's essential. Establish a pre-sleep ritual that tells your body it's time to hit the hay—whether that's a warm bath, reading a book, or some gentle stretches. Consistency is key. Going to bed and waking up at the same time every day (yes, even on weekends) helps regulate your body's internal clock, making it easier to fall asleep and wake up naturally.

But what if, despite your best efforts, sleep remains elusive? Enter common sleep disorders like insomnia and sleep apnea. Insomnia, where you have trouble falling or staying asleep, can be triggered by stress, lifestyle habits, or even your diet. Sleep apnea, on the other hand, is a more serious condition where your breathing stops and starts throughout the night, severely disrupting your sleep. These aren't just minor nuisances; they can significantly impair your quality of life and health. If you suspect you might have a sleep disorder, don't just toss and turn in despair. Seek professional help. Often, these conditions can be managed effectively with the right interventions, from lifestyle changes to medical treatment.

Lastly, let's connect the dots between sleep and decision-making. Research has consistently shown that a well-rested brain performs significantly better in tasks that require cognitive function. Sleep affects your reasoning, problem-solving skills, and ability to maintain attention. Ever noticed how everything seems more challenging when you're tired? That's because sleep deprivation clouds your decision-making processes and emotional responses. In contrast, a good night's sleep enhances your brain's ability to assess situations accurately and react more judiciously.

So, as we explore the landscapes of personal development and self-care, let's not undervalue the profound impact of sleep. It's not just about preventing grogginess; it's about setting the stage for a healthier, more effective, and enjoyable life. Let's make sleep a priority, not an afterthought, because every good day starts the night before.

6.4 Stress-Relieving Physical Activities That Boost Performance

Let's dive into a topic that's close to my heart and essential for keeping our sanity intact—stress-relieving physical activities. Now, we're not talking about the occasional frantic sprint to catch a bus. Nope, this is about intentional, enjoyable activities that not only kick stress to the curb but also pump up your performance in all areas of life. Think swimming, running, and cycling. Imagine the last time you took a dip in the pool, went for a jog, or hopped on a bike. Remember that exhilarating feeling of wind in your hair and worries slipping away? That's not just joy—it's science at work!

Swimming, for starters, is like giving your body and mind a spa day. Immersed in water, every stroke you take not only builds muscle but also burns away the mental load. The rhythmic nature of swimming and the sensation of being buoyed by water can significantly reduce physical and mental stress. It's not just about the physical act of swimming but also about being in a serene, blue space. It's calming, meditative, and a potent antidote to the high-octane hustle of daily life.

Running, on the other hand, might seem daunting to some. But here's the kicker: it's one of the most effective ways to slash stress levels. When you run, your body releases endorphins, often touted as the body's natural painkillers. But these nifty little hormones are also your personal stress-busters. They improve your mood, clear your mind, and can even provide a feeling of euphoria, commonly known as the 'runner's high'. Whether it's a scenic trail run or a quick jog around your neighborhood, the impact is the same—a happier, less stressed you.

Cycling combines the physical benefits of exercise with the emotional relief of being outside and exploring new vistas. Pedaling through streets or nature trails can be incredibly liberating, offering a sense of freedom and escape from everyday pressures. It's not only good for your legs but also for your soul. Plus, as you focus on your route and your rhythm, cycling offers a wonderful way to clear your mind and sharpen your focus.

Now, the benefits of regular engagement in these activities extend far beyond the immediate relief they provide. Physiologically, exercises like swimming, running, and cycling help lower cortisol and adrenaline levels—your body's stress hormones. This reduction not only helps you feel calmer and more relaxed but also protects your body from the long-term effects of stress, which can include everything from headaches to heart disease. Regular physical activity strengthens your heart, improves your circulation, and increases your overall energy levels, making you more resilient both physically and mentally.

Incorporating these activities into your daily routine might seem challenging, especially when your calendar is bursting at the seams. However, the trick is to weave them into your day so seamlessly that they become a natural part of your life, not another task on your to-do list. Start small; perhaps a 15-minute walk or cycle to work. Gradually increase the duration as it becomes a fixed part of your routine. If you're pressed for time, consider high-intensity interval training (HIIT) versions of swimming or running that pack maximum benefits into minimal time.

To give you a real-world sense of how transformative these activities can be, let's talk about Linda. A software developer who faced deadlines daily, Linda started cycling to work instead of driving. Initially, it was just a way to sneak in some exercise, but she soon noticed a significant drop in her stress levels. Her focus sharpened, her productivity soared, and her evenings became more relaxed. Linda's story isn't unique; it's achievable for anyone willing to step up and move.

So, why not give it a shot? Swap the elevator for stairs, the car for a bike, or the couch for a swim. Your body (and your boss) will thank you as you turn stress into sweat, one day at a time. Remember, every step, stroke, or pedal gets you closer to a healthier, more vibrant version of yourself. Now, let's keep moving forward, exploring more ways to enhance our personal development and self-care.

6.5 The Role of Nutrition in Cognitive Function

Let's bite into a topic that's as tasty as it is transformative—nutrition and its profound impact on your brain's horsepower. Have you ever considered that what you eat doesn't just fuel your body but also feeds your brain? Yep, every forkful of food can be a step toward sharper thinking, better memory, and even a sunnier mood. So, put on your chef's hat, because we're about to cook up some delicious strategies for keeping your mental gears greased.

First up, the building blocks of brain health: nutrients like omega-3 fatty acids, antioxidants, and essential vitamins. These aren't just fancy buzzwords; they're the VIPs at the party inside your skull. Omega-3 fatty acids, found aplenty in fish like salmon, sardines, and even in flaxseeds and walnuts, are like the oil in your car—they keep the engine running smoothly. They help build and repair brain cells, and studies suggest they may slow age-related mental decline and help ward off Alzheimer's disease. Then there are antioxidants—these little warriors fight against oxidative stress that contributes to brain aging and cognitive decline. You'll find them gallivanting generously in berries, leafy greens, nuts, and seeds. And let's not forget about B vitamins, found in whole grains, meats, eggs, and legumes; they are crucial for creating neurotransmitters and can bolster brain function.

Now, how about we talk eating patterns? Ever heard of the Mediterranean diet? It's like the all-star team of diets for brain health. Rich in vegetables, fruits, nuts, whole grains, fish, and using olive oil galore, it's a diet that not only sings to your taste buds but also serenades your neurons. This diet is low in red meat and dairy, which aligns perfectly with the need to reduce saturated fats—a known culprit in cognitive decline. By sticking to this diet, you're not only setting the table for a healthier heart but also prepping your brain to stay as sharp as a Michelin-star chef's knife.

But here's the kicker—eating right can also be your secret weapon against cognitive decline. It's like armor for your gray matter. Foods high in compounds like flavonoids and omega-3s (think dark chocolate and fatty fish) are not just delicious; they also provide a buffer against the wear and tear of aging. Incorporating these foods into your diet can help maintain brain function as you clock up the birthdays, keeping those 'senior moments' at bay.

Let's get practical with some meal planning tips that don't just flirt with your taste buds but also feed your brain. Imagine starting your day with a smoothie bowl packed with berries, a sprinkle of flaxseeds, and a handful of nuts. For lunch, how about a quinoa and grilled salmon salad drizzled with olive oil and lemon? And for dinner, a vibrant stir-fry with heaps of veggies, tossed in a tad of olive oil and served with a side of whole-grain bread. Here's a pro tip: prep your meals in advance to avoid the "what's for dinner?" brain drain and keep your eating habits on track without last-minute decisions leading you astray.

Through mindful nutrition, you're not just eating; you're curating a menu for a well-oiled brain. Every meal is an opportunity to enhance your mental clarity, boost your memory, and keep your thoughts as crisp as a fresh salad. So, let's keep making mealtime a time to re-energize, not just your body but your brain too. With every bite, remember, you're feeding your greatest asset. Let's make every meal count, for your body's health and your brain's brilliance.

6.6 Meditation and Yoga: Tools for Inner Peace and Focus

Let's roll out the yoga mat and settle into the world of meditation and yoga, where each breath and stretch can lead you to a sanctuary of calm and focus. These ancient practices aren't just about twisting into pretzels or sitting quietly with your thoughts—they are powerful tools that can enhance your mental, physical, and emotional well-being. Whether you're a bustling executive or a busy parent, incorporating these practices into your life can be a game-changer, offering a wellspring of energy and serenity amidst the chaos of daily life.

Basics of Meditation and Yoga

Meditation and yoga are often spoken about in the same breath, and for a good reason. Both practices emphasize mindfulness and are rooted in the art of maintaining presence and awareness. While yoga incorporates physical postures and breathing techniques, meditation generally involves a focus on breath, a phrase, or a calming sound to achieve mental clarity and emotional calmness. The beauty of these practices lies in their simplicity and the profound impact they can have on your life, helping to reduce stress, improve concentration, and enhance overall well-being.

For beginners, the thought of starting a meditation or yoga practice can seem daunting—visions of monks sitting in serene silence or limber yogis twisting into impossible shapes. But here's the good news: both practices can be incredibly flexible and adapted to fit any lifestyle or skill level. You can start small, with just a few minutes a day, and gradually increase the time as you become more comfortable with the techniques.

Techniques for Beginners

Starting a meditation practice can be as simple as dedicating five minutes each morning or evening to sit in a quiet space and focus on your breathing. Find a comfortable seat, close your eyes, and breathe naturally. Focus your attention on the breath and on how the body moves with each inhalation and exhalation. If your mind wanders, simply bring your focus back to your breath without judgment. Over time, this practice can help you develop a sharper focus and reduce everyday stress.

Yoga, meanwhile, doesn't require you to be ultra-flexible or own fancy equipment. You can begin with basic poses like the mountain pose, where you stand straight with your feet together and arms at your sides, focusing on your breathing and the alignment of your body. Or try the downward-facing dog, a fundamental pose that stretches and strengthens many parts of the body. Yoga routines can be found in books, on-line videos, or apps that guide you through sequences at various levels of difficulty.

Incorporating Mindfulness into Daily Life

The true magic of meditation and yoga shines when you integrate the mindfulness learned on the mat into your daily life. It could be as simple as being fully present while eating, walking, or even during conversations. This practice of mindfulness can help you maintain a calm, clear mind throughout the day, enhancing your focus and productivity. It's about making every action intentional and being fully present in the moment, which can transform mundane tasks into moments of zen.

Scientific Research Supporting Benefits

The benefits of meditation and yoga are not just anecdotal; numerous scientific studies back them up. Research has shown that regular meditation can decrease cortisol levels, thus reducing stress. It can also improve concentration, memory, and the ability to multitask. Yoga has been found to improve flexibility, balance, and strength while significantly reducing symptoms of anxiety and depression. These practices have also been linked to better sleep patterns and enhanced overall health, making them a powerhouse duo for anyone looking to boost their mental and physical health.

As we wrap up this exploration into meditation and yoga, remember that the journey into these practices is personal and can be tailored to fit your lifestyle and needs. Whether you're looking for a way to cope with stress, enhance your focus, or simply find a moment of peace in your hectic day, meditation and yoga can offer you the tools you need. So, take a deep breath, and let's embrace these ancient practices that have improved the lives of millions around the globe.

Now, as we turn the page from exploring inward practices to understanding our interactions with others, let's carry forward the tranquility and focus we've cultivated here. In the next chapter, we'll dive into how effective communication and managing relationships play a pivotal role in personal and professional success, using the foundations of mindfulness to enhance every interaction.

Part 2

Chapter 7: Building and Sustaining Relationships

Imagine walking into a room where every handshake is a potential new chapter, every smile a foot in the door to new opportunities. Welcome to the art of networking—the unsung hero in the saga of professional success. It's not just about collecting business cards like Pokémon; it's about weaving the fabric of your career, one relationship at a time. Let's dive into the nitty-gritty of networking strategies that can transform you from a wallflower to a master weaver of professional ties.

7.1 Networking Strategies for the Modern Professional

Leveraging Social Media for Networking

In the digital age, platforms like LinkedIn are not just your resume; they are your digital handshake. To network effectively on platforms like these, think of your profile as your personal billboard. It needs to be eye-catching, informative, and reflective of your professional persona. Start by sprucing up your profile with a professional photo— yes, that means no beach selfies. Then, craft a compelling headline and summary that not only outline your skills but also hint at your career aspirations. It's like telling a story where you're both the protagonist and the narrator.

Now, posting on LinkedIn isn't just about sharing your latest coffee run. It's about sharing insights, celebrating achievements (yours and others'), and starting conversations. Share articles relevant to your industry with thoughtful commentary, or better yet, write your own posts. This isn't just about visibility—it's about showcasing your expertise and interests. Engaging with others' content is equally crucial. Comment with insightful observations or supportive feedback. It's like saying, "Hey, I'm here, I'm interested, and I've got ideas too."

Attending and Making the Most of Events

Remember, every event you attend is more than just free snacks and branded pens. It's a treasure trove of potential connections. But here's the kicker—you need to be selective. Choose events that align with your career goals or passions. Once you're there, have a game plan. Set a goal for how many people you want to meet, and don't just stick to familiar faces. Be the one to break the ice; have your elevator pitch polished and ready to roll out. It doesn't have to be a dry recital of your resume—make it a catchy, engaging snippet of who you are and what you're passionate about.

Engaging in conversations at these events is an art. Be genuinely interested in what others have to say. Ask questions, listen actively, and see where you can add value. Maybe it's a piece of advice, a book recommendation, or an introduction to someone else. Networking is a two-way street; think about how you can help others, not just what you can get out of the interaction.

Building Lasting Professional Relationships

Networking isn't a hit-and-run game. The real magic happens in the follow-up. After the event, reach out with a personalized message—perhaps mentioning something specific you discussed. It shows you were paying attention and value the connection. But don't just reach out when you need a favor. Keep the relationship warm by checking in periodically, sharing relevant articles, or congratulating them on professional milestones. It's like watering a plant; regular care keeps it thriving.

Using Networking for Career Advancement

Strategic networking can propel your career to new heights. It's about positioning yourself in the right circles and being proactive. Identify leaders in your field or potential mentors and find ways to connect—whether through introductions, social media, or industry events. Once you've established a connection, don't be shy about expressing your career aspirations. Ask for advice, feedback, or even if they know of any opportunities. Remember, if you don't ask, the answer is always no.

In the grand chess game of your career, networking is your power move. It opens doors, creates opportunities, and builds bridges to places you might not reach alone. So, step out of your comfort zone, reach out with confidence, and weave your web of professional relationships. Who knows where your next handshake will lead you?

7.2 Mentorship: Finding Guidance and Providing It

Navigating the professional world can sometimes feel like trying to solve a Rubik's Cube blindfolded. This is where a mentor can turn into your professional life-saver, offering you the glasses to see the colors clearly. The perks of having a mentor are profound: accelerated learning, navigating through career hurdles with less stumbling, and expanding your professional network in ways that are often not possible on your own. Think of a mentor as a GPS system when you are at crossroads; not only can they suggest which route might be quicker or more scenic, but they can also foresee the potholes you need to avoid.

Finding the right mentor, however, is where many hit a snag. It's not about finding someone with a flashy title or a corner office, but finding someone whose career path resonates with your aspirations and whose insights align with your needs. Start by identifying what you want to achieve in your career and what skills you need to develop. Attend industry conferences, seminars, and other networking events where potential mentors might frequent. Engage in discussions, participate in forums, and when you spot a potential mentor, approach them with a specific ask. For instance, after a panel discussion, you might approach a panelist with, "I really admired your insights on sustainable business practices. Could I get your advice on a project I'm working on that aligns with this theme?" It's about creating a connection based on mutual interests and respect.

Being an effective mentee is an art in itself. It requires humility, openness, and a bit of courage. Always come prepared to meetings with your mentor. Have a list of topics or questions you want to discuss. Show that you value their time by being punctual and focused during your interactions. Remember, this is a two-way relationship. Make sure to keep your mentor updated on your progress and how their advice has helped you. Small gestures, like a thank-you note or a quick update email, can go a long way in showing your appreciation and keeping the relationship strong.

Transitioning from being mentored to becoming a mentor can feel like a cap and gown moment—graduating to a new level in your professional life. When you decide to take on this role, reflect on what made your mentors effective. Was it their ability to listen, their insightful feedback, or their encouragement to push boundaries? Use these reflections to shape your own mentoring style. Start by offering to mentor someone in your organization or volunteer for mentoring programs in your professional community. Share your experiences, the good and the bad. Be honest about your failures and how you overcame them. This vulnerability not only humanizes you but also deepens the learning experience for your mentee.

In essence, mentorship is about passing on the wisdom you've gathered along your journey and learning from others, no matter which side of the mentor-mentee relationship you are on. It's a dynamic of give and take that can significantly sculpt your professional landscape and theirs. So, as you progress in your career, keep the cycle of guidance and learning rotating, because every interaction is a step forward for someone, possibly even yourself.

7.3 The Dynamics of Teamwork: Making the Most of Collective Strengths

Think of the most memorable sports teams in history; what made them unforgettable wasn't just their individual talents, but how they functioned seamlessly together, like a well-oiled machine. The same dynamic applies to workplace teams. Understanding the roles each member plays, akin to positions on a sports team, can dramatically enhance performance and project outcomes. One insightful model that helps in deciphering these roles is Belbin's Team Roles. This framework categorizes team roles into nine types, such as the Plant, who is creative and good at solving complex problems, and the Implementer, who gets things done. Knowing who excels at what can help in assigning tasks that align perfectly with each member's intrinsic strengths, thereby not just optimizing productivity but also increasing job satisfaction.

Imagine you're leading a project with a diverse group; someone has to brainstorm the big ideas, another has to scrutinize the details, while someone else ensures the deadlines are met. By applying Belbin's model, you can delegate responsibilities that play to each member's strengths. The Plant would be fantastic at throwing out innovative ideas, the Monitor Evaluator could assess the feasibility of these ideas, and the Completer Finisher would ensure no detail is missed in the execution. It's about creating a symphony where each player knows their part to perfection.

Now, fostering a collaborative environment is much more than just putting people together in a room and telling them to 'work together'. It requires cultivating a culture of collaboration and respect. This starts with open lines of communication. Encourage team members to voice their ideas and concerns openly without fear of judgment. This could be through regular team meetings or brainstorming sessions where everyone is encouraged to speak up. Conflict is inevitable, but how it's handled can make or break the team dynamic. Equip your team with conflict resolution tools that emphasize empathy, active listening, and finding mutually beneficial solutions. Regular team-building activities can also strengthen bonds and improve collaborative efforts. These don't always have to be big outings; even small, consistent activities like shared lunch breaks or quick team huddles can boost morale and foster a sense of unity.

Leveraging diversity within teams is another cornerstone of high-performance teams. Each team member brings a unique set of skills, experiences, and perspectives that can enrich the team's output. A diverse team can approach problems from various angles, leading to more innovative solutions. However, this diversity needs to be actively managed to prevent miscommunications and conflicts. Encourage team members to share their backgrounds and professional experiences. Organize training sessions that highlight the importance of diversity and teach ways to harness it. For instance, a workshop on cultural competence can open eyes to new ways of communication and interaction that respect everyone's background.

Analyzing case studies of successful teams can provide valuable lessons in teamwork dynamics. Take the example of a tech company that managed to bring a groundbreaking product to market in record time. Their secret? A cross-functional team that broke down silos and combined the expertise of engineers, marketers, and customer service representatives. This integration enabled real-time feedback and faster iterations, significantly reducing the product's time to market. Another case could be a healthcare provider that improved patient satisfaction scores through an interdisciplinary team approach, where doctors, nurses, and administrative staff worked together to streamline the patient experience. These examples underscore the power of well-orchestrated teamwork that leverages diverse competencies and fosters a culture of collaboration and respect.

Building an effective team is like directing a choir; each member has a unique voice, but it's the harmony they create together that leaves an impact. By understanding and implementing strategic team roles, fostering a collaborative environment, and embracing diversity, you can orchestrate a team that not only performs well but also enjoys the process, leading to sustainable success and innovation.

7.4 Managing Relationship Expectations: Family, Friends, and Partners

Navigating the complexities of relationships—be it with family, friends, or partners—is akin to being a seasoned chef in a gourmet kitchen. Just as a chef adjusts ingredients to perfect a dish, managing relationships often involves adjusting expectations to maintain harmony and satisfaction. You see, setting clear and realistic expectations isn't just about avoiding disappointments; it's about creating a foundation of understanding and respect that can elevate every relationship in your life.

Let's start with the basics: setting expectations. Picture this: you're planning a weekend getaway with friends. By discussing and agreeing on what each person anticipates from the trip—relaxation, adventure, or perhaps a culinary exploration—you set the stage for a successful experience. The same principle applies to more significant life scenarios, such as moving in with a partner or sharing business responsibilities with a friend. Effective communication is key. It's about being honest and upfront about what you expect from each other. This might mean having uncomfortable conversations or admitting to vulnerabilities, but it's these discussions that prevent misunderstandings and build stronger bonds. Tools like 'expectation lists'—where each person writes down what they expect from the other in various situations—can be incredibly useful. It's a practical way to visually map out where alignments and gaps exist, allowing both parties to navigate the relationship more thoughtfully.

Balancing personal and professional life is another tightrope walk most of us face. Let's say you're a career-driven individual who also values family time. Here, setting boundaries is crucial. It might involve negotiating work hours that don't encroach on family dinners or dedicating weekends exclusively to personal time. Technology, while a facilitator, can also blur these lines. Establish tech-free zones or times at home where work calls or emails are off-limits, fostering quality family interactions. On the flip side, communicate these boundaries clearly at your workplace. It's about managing expectations on both fronts, ensuring neither sphere feels neglected. Remember, it's not about giving equal time to both, but about giving sufficient and meaningful time to each.

Disappointments and misunderstandings, though painful, are inevitable. Perhaps a friend forgets an important event or a partner isn't supportive in a moment of need. Handling these situations with grace involves first managing your own emotions. Take a step back and assess why the situation hurts and how it deviates from your expectations. Then, approach the conversation with a goal of understanding, not accusation. Use "I feel" statements to express your feelings without blame. For instance, saying, "I felt hurt when you didn't support my decision because it made me feel undervalued," clearly communicates your feelings without casting blame. This opens up a dialogue that fosters understanding and healing, rather than conflict.

Finally, as life evolves, so do relationships. The expectations you had in your twenties may not hold in your forties. Regular 'relationship audits' can be beneficial. This involves sitting down with those you have close relationships with and revisiting your expectations, boundaries, and shared goals. Life events such as a new job, a baby, or even personal growth can shift priorities and capabilities. Embrace these changes by adjusting your expectations accordingly. This not only prevents feelings of resentment but also deepens the relationship through continued alignment and mutual support.

In essence, managing relationship expectations is about continual communication, adaptation, and mutual understanding. It's a dynamic dance that requires patience, empathy, and occasionally, the courage to redefine the steps you take together. By mastering this dance, you not only enhance your personal happiness but also forge deeper and more enduring connections.

7.5 Repairing Damaged Relationships: Steps Toward Reconciliation

When the warm glow of a friendship dims or the steady flame of a partnership flickers, it's tempting to either let the fire die out or to douse it with a bucket of icy dismissal. Yet, not all strained relationships deserve a cold end; some just need a bit of rekindling. Recognizing when a relationship is worth salvaging is akin to being a relationship detective. You need to look for clues that suggest a fundamentally healthy relationship beneath the temporary chaos. Signs like mutual respect, shared values, and genuine affection are like green lights on your dashboard, indicating that despite current issues, the foundation is solid. On the flip side, constant disrespect, lack of trust, and emotional drain are red flags, signaling a toxic dynamic that might not be worth your energy. It's crucial to differentiate between a relationship going through a rough patch and one that's fundamentally flawed.

Suppose you've identified a relationship that's dented but not doomed. The next step is initiating reconciliation, which can feel like walking a tightrope over a canyon—intimidating yet thrilling. The key to starting this conversation is choosing the right moment and approach. You want to talk when both parties are calm and unlikely to be interrupted. Begin with expressing your intention to mend things, which shows you're invested in the relationship's health. A simple, "I've been thinking about how we left things, and I feel it's important for us to clear the air," can open the dialogue without immediate blame.

Apologizing effectively is an art. It's not just about saying "I'm sorry"; it's about articulating what you're sorry for and acknowledging the impact of your actions. This shows a deep level of understanding and remorse, which can soften hardened feelings and pave the way for healing. For instance, instead of a generic apology, you might say, "I'm sorry for raising my voice during our last conversation. I can only imagine how disrespected that made you feel, and that was not my intention." This kind of apology not only expresses regret but also validates the other person's feelings, which is crucial for rebuilding trust.

Forgiveness is the bridge that connects confrontation with reconciliation. It's about letting go of the bitterness to make room for healing. Embracing forgiveness doesn't mean forgetting what happened or excusing unacceptable behavior; rather, it's about freeing yourself from the burden of resentment. Discuss the importance of forgiveness, not just as a gift to the other person but as a salve for your own emotional wounds. Encourage open dialogue about what each party needs to move forward. This might involve setting new boundaries or commitments to prevent past grievances from repeating. Building trust takes time, and it's often in these post-conflict resolutions that relationships find new depths, strengthened by the mutual effort to overcome hardships.

Sometimes, the tangle of emotions and past hurts can be too complex to unravel alone. This is when professional help can be invaluable. Seeking assistance from a counselor or mediator can provide a neutral ground for airing grievances and finding solutions. This step is especially beneficial in situations where communication has broken down significantly or where the issues at hand are particularly sensitive, such as in cases of betrayal or deep-seated resentment. Professionals can guide the conversation in a productive direction, ensuring that both parties feel heard and respected throughout the reconciliation process.

Navigating the choppy waters of relationship repair requires courage, patience, and a willingness to delve into uncomfortable emotional territories. Whether it's a friendship that's drifted, a family feud, or a romantic relationship on the rocks, taking steps toward reconciliation can lead to a renewed connection that's even stronger than before. Remember, the goal isn't just to go back to how things were but to build a new, healthier dynamic that can withstand the tests of time and change.

7.6 Social Skills for the Introverted

Let's debunk a common myth right off the bat: Introversion isn't about being shy or antisocial. Instead, think of introversion as your unique superpower in the social realm, particularly because of the depth and authenticity introverts bring to interactions. Introverts often excel in environments where they can form deep, meaningful connections, rather than surface-level schmoozing. So, if the idea of networking events sends a shiver down your spine, fear not. There are strategies that play to your strengths and allow you to navigate these waters without draining your energy reserves.

Firstly, tailor your networking approach to favor quality over quantity. Instead of trying to meet everyone in the room, focus on forming a few meaningful connections. When you engage in conversations, dive deeper. Ask open-ended questions that invite a detailed response, and really listen. This not only makes the conversation more interesting for you but also makes the person you're speaking to feel valued and understood. It's about creating a mini-environment where genuine interest replaces small talk. For introverts, such interactions can be more rewarding and less exhausting, providing a sense of accomplishment rather than depletion.

Managing your social energy is crucial. Networking events or social gatherings can often feel like marathons for introverts. The key is recognizing your energy limits and planning accordingly. One effective strategy is the "intermission approach." Plan to step out for a few minutes halfway through the event to recharge. This could mean finding a quiet corner, stepping outside, or simply taking a moment to breathe and gather your thoughts. These short breaks can prevent the overwhelming exhaustion that might otherwise make you want to flee at the halfway point.

Setting comfortable boundaries is also essential. It's okay to be upfront about your preferences. If you're more comfortable with one-on-one meetings, suggest catching up over coffee instead of at a bustling happy hour. When you shape the social setting in a way that respects your energy levels, you transform networking from a dreaded chore into an enjoyable activity. Remember, if you're at ease, you're more likely to make a positive impression.

Building confidence in social settings often begins long before you enter a room full of people. Preparation can significantly reduce anxiety. Before an event, arm yourself with knowledge about the topics likely to be discussed, the guests who might attend, and the context of the gathering. This preparation allows you to feel more secure in your ability to contribute meaningfully to conversations. Additionally, rehearse a few icebreakers or questions you could ask. Something as simple as, "What's the most interesting project you've worked on this year?" can open up a dialogue in a way that feels natural and engaging.

Another confidence booster is the realization that you don't have to change who you are to fit into the social mold. Embrace your introversion as a part of your unique professional persona. Many people appreciate the thoughtful, calm nature that introverts often bring to conversations. By owning your introverted qualities, you project a level of self-assurance that is both refreshing and attractive in a business context.

To sum up, navigating social landscapes as an introvert doesn't require you to shout the loudest or schmooze the most. It's about leveraging your natural propensity for deep conversation, managing your energy wisely, and setting the stage for interactions that leave you energized rather than depleted. By embracing these strategies, you not only preserve your authentic self but also turn your introversion into a powerful tool in building meaningful professional relationships.

As we wrap up this exploration into the nuanced world of social interactions for introverts, remember that each conversation, each connection, is a step toward not just professional success but personal growth. The skills you cultivate in these interactions extend beyond networking—they enrich every facet of your life, enhancing your communication, empathy, and understanding in a world that deeply values connection.

Shifting gears, the next chapter will delve into another critical aspect of professional and personal development: mastering the art of negotiation. Just as we've seen how understanding and leveraging one's personality traits in social settings can lead to more meaningful interactions, we'll explore how negotiation, when approached with the right strategies, can lead to successful outcomes in various aspects of life.

Part 2

Chapter 8 Advancing Your Career

Imagine stepping into a crowded market, where every stall is vying for attention with vibrant colors and enticing aromas. Now, picture your career in such a marketplace. How do you ensure that your stall, your professional identity, stands out? This is where the magic of personal branding comes into play, transforming you from just another face in the crowd to the one everyone wants to know. Let's dive into how you can craft a professional identity that not only shines but also resonates deeply within your industry.

8.1 Personal Branding: Crafting Your Professional Identity

Defining Personal Branding

Think of personal branding as your own unique fragrance that lingers even after you've left the room. It's the essence of who you are professionally and how you broadcast that identity to the world. Why is it crucial, you ask? Well, in a competitive job market, a strong personal brand distinguishes you from your counterparts, much like a master chef known for a signature dish. It's about more than just skills and experiences; it's about your values, your story, and how effectively you communicate these elements across various platforms.

Developing a Unique Value Proposition

Your unique value proposition (UVP) is akin to a secret sauce in your professional toolkit. It's what makes you, you; it's why a company would choose to invest in you over anyone else. To refine your UVP, start by identifying your unique strengths and the specific benefits these strengths offer to an employer or client. Are you a tech wizard who can increase operational efficiency through automation? Or perhaps a marketing maestro capable of doubling an audience through innovative strategies? Once you pinpoint your strengths, weave them into a compelling narrative. Remember, your UVP should answer the crucial question: "Why you?"

Building an On-line Presence

In today's digital world, your on-line presence can be your strongest ally or your greatest foe in the quest to establish a robust personal brand. Platforms like LinkedIn, professional blogs, or even your own website serve as your virtual billboards. To optimize these platforms, ensure your profiles are not only complete but also compelling. Use professional photos, engage regularly by sharing industry-related content, and contribute your own articles or insights to establish thought leadership. Each post, comment, or share is a brushstroke in the larger picture of your professional identity.

Consistency Across All Platforms

The key to effective personal branding? Consistency. Imagine if every Coca-Cola bottle looked different; would it be as iconic? Unlikely. Similarly, your professional materials—be it on LinkedIn, your personal blog, or even business cards—should all tell a cohesive story. This consistency in messaging and appearance helps build familiarity and trust. It ensures that whether a potential employer scrolls through your Twitter, checks out your LinkedIn, or lands on your blog, they receive the same compelling narrative about who you are and what you stand for.

So, let's get your brand out there! Start by revising your LinkedIn headline, spruce up that old blog post, or perhaps give your resume a fresh new look aligned with your brand. Remember, in the grand marketplace of careers, your personal brand is your loudest hailer. Make it count.

With your newfound understanding of personal branding, you're well-equipped to navigate the complexities of the professional world with confidence and clarity. As you continue to refine and broadcast your brand, remember that it's an ongoing process. Your professional identity will evolve as you grow and learn, so revisit and update your materials regularly to ensure they reflect the person you are becoming. This proactive approach will not only help you maintain relevance but also ensure that your personal brand continues to resonate with your evolving career goals.

8.2 Career Transitions: When and How to Make Your Move

Imagine waking up one morning and realizing that the job you once leaped out of bed for now barely gets a snooze button's worth of excitement. Maybe the projects that used to spark your creativity now flicker out faster than a cheap candle. That's your professional intuition nudging you, suggesting it might be time for a change. Recognizing the right moment to shift gears in your career isn't always about glaring issues; sometimes, it's the subtle signs, like the slow fade of passion or the constant feeling that you're capable of more. Perhaps opportunities for advancement have dried up, or the learning curve has flattened into a straight line. These are your cues that a career transition might not just be an option but a necessity.

Now, deciding to switch careers is like deciding to climb a mountain—it's thrilling, yes, but without a map and a solid plan, you might just end up going around in circles. Planning your career transition should be approached with the precision of a master chess player. Start by identifying the skills you need to develop or sharpen. This might mean going back to school for advanced training or certification, or it might be as simple as taking on-line courses to beef up areas like digital literacy or project management.

Next up, industry research. This is where you transform into a detective of sorts. Dive into the industry you're eyeing. Who are the major players? What trends are shaping its future? What skills are in high demand? Informational interviews can be gold here. Reach out to folks already working in the field. Most people love to share their insights and can provide you with the insider scoop on what it's really like to work in that space.

Financial planning cannot be overlooked because let's face it, bills don't pay themselves. Transitioning careers might involve some financial downtime, so having a runway is crucial. How long can you go without a steady income? Do you have savings to cover this period? Maybe you need to tighten the budget belt for a while. Planning financially cushions the stress and lets you focus on your career goals without the distraction of financial strain.

Executing a career transition smoothly is akin to conducting an orchestra—every move needs to be harmonized. Activating your network is like bringing in the violin section. Reach out to former colleagues, join professional groups, attend industry conferences— start making waves in your new professional pond. When it comes to resigning from your current role, think strategic retreat rather than abrupt exit. A graceful notice period, thorough handover, and maintaining positive relationships can turn former colleagues into future allies.

As you step into your new role or industry, remember, first impressions are more like fresh cement—quick to take shape. Early on, demonstrate your commitment and capabilities. Be proactive in taking on projects, eager to learn, and quick to integrate. Show up with not just the skills but also the enthusiasm that says you're there to make a difference. Seek out quick wins—small but impactful projects that you can turn around swiftly to establish your reputation as someone who gets things done.

Navigating a career change is no small feat—it requires guts, strategy, and a touch of finesse. But with the right approach, each step can be a stepping stone to a career that not only challenges you but also brings back that spark that got you jumping out of bed in the first place. So, take that leap, make your move, and let the professional adventure begin.

8.3 Advanced Networking: Leveraging Your Contacts for Opportunities

Think of networking not just as a skill but as a superpower in your career toolkit. While many of us are familiar with the basics—handshakes, business cards, and the occasional LinkedIn message—the real magic happens when you step up your game to advanced networking. This isn't about padding your contacts list with as many names as possible; it's about cultivating deeper, mutually beneficial relationships that can truly transform your career trajectory.

Let's break down what this means in practice. Advanced networking is akin to being a community gardener; it's about nurturing relationships with care, precision, and a genuine interest in mutual growth. It starts with strategic relationship management. Picture your network as a garden where different plants represent different contacts. Just like in gardening, you need to know which plants need more sunlight (more frequent check-ins) and which thrive in the shade (less maintenance). Begin by categorizing your contacts based on how closely they align with your career objectives and personal values. This might mean grouping them into categories such as thought leaders, industry peers, potential mentors, and newcomers. Each group requires a different approach and frequency of interaction, ensuring that you invest the right amount of energy without spreading yourself too thin.

Now, leveraging technology in networking isn't just about being active on social media; it's about using these platforms strategically to foster genuine connections. Use tools like LinkedIn not only to post updates but to engage meaningfully with others' content. Comment with insightful thoughts, ask questions, and share posts that align with your professional ethos. Platforms like Twitter can be used to join industry-specific conversations or chats, which can increase your visibility and position you as an engaged member of your field. Remember, the goal is to provide value, whether it's sharing a relevant article, highlighting someone else's work, or offering your unique perspective on a hot topic.

But how do you turn these cultivated relationships into tangible opportunities? It starts by identifying synergies—areas where your interests and the interests of your contacts overlap. This could be a shared passion for sustainable business practices, a common alumni network, or a mutual interest in technological innovations. Once you identify these commonalities, you can propose collaborations that are beneficial for both parties. This could look like co-authoring a white paper, organizing a panel discussion, or starting a podcast series. These initiatives not only strengthen your relationship by working towards a common goal but also enhance your visibility and credibility within your industry.

Asking for introductions is another powerful tool in your networking arsenal. If you know someone who can connect you to a person you're eager to meet, don't hesitate to ask for an introduction—but always be tactful and respectful. Make it easy for your contact by providing a brief blurb they can use to introduce you, and always explain why you value the introduction. This approach shows professionalism and respect for both your existing contact's and the new contact's time and energy.

By taking your networking efforts to the next level, you transform simple connections into career-accelerating partnerships and opportunities. Remember, advanced networking is less about collecting contacts and more about cultivating meaningful relationships and opportunities that benefit all involved. It's a dynamic, ongoing process that can significantly shape your professional path, so invest in it wisely, nurture it with care, and watch as it blossoms into a thriving ecosystem of professional growth and opportunities.

8.4 The Role of Creativity and Innovation in Career Advancement

Imagine your career as a canvas. Every brushstroke represents a skill, experience, or achievement. Now, what happens when you add a splash of creativity and a dash of innovation to this picture? Suddenly, your canvas isn't just interesting—it's captivating, it's dynamic, it's a masterpiece that stands out in the gallery of professional achievements. Fostering a creative mindset isn't just about thinking outside the box; it's about realizing that the box was never necessary to begin with. Engaging with diverse disciplines, continuously learning, and embracing experimentation are not just activities; they're your tools for sculpting a career that's as innovative as it is impressive.

Think about the times when you've stepped into a role or a project that seemed routine. Now, consider how approaching it with a fresh perspective or a novel idea could transform the mundane into the extraordinary. This is where creativity becomes your career booster. For instance, imagine you're in marketing and tasked with an ordinary campaign. By integrating technology differently, say, using augmented reality to provide customers with a virtual experience of your product, you've not only enhanced the campaign's appeal but also set a benchmark in your company for innovative thinking.

Now, while creativity is the spark, innovation is the engine that drives your career forward. Bringing innovative solutions to the workplace doesn't just solve problems more efficiently; it also elevates your visibility among peers and superiors. It positions you as a thought leader, someone capable of steering the ship through uncharted waters. Whether it's streamlining processes to save costs or introducing a new product line that opens up additional revenue streams, innovation underscores your value to the organization.

But how do you consistently come up with these groundbreaking ideas? This is where tools and methodologies like design thinking and lateral thinking come into play. Design thinking, with its empathetic and user-centered approach, can help you develop solutions that not only meet the needs but also enhance the experiences of your customers or colleagues. It's about understanding the human element in every problem—what frustrates people, what delights them, and then designing solutions from this empathetic perspective. Lateral thinking, on the other hand, is your tool for breaking conventional patterns of thinking. It encourages looking at problems from different angles, asking 'what if' and 'why not', which can lead to surprising and innovative solutions that a straightforward approach might miss.

Implementing these innovative ideas in the workplace, however, is where many stumble. It's one thing to have a great idea, but another to see it realized. Securing buy-in from stakeholders is crucial and can be achieved by demonstrating the tangible benefits of your innovation, be it enhancing efficiency, reducing costs, or boosting sales. Start small with pilot testing; this not only minimizes risk but also allows you to gather concrete data to support your idea. For example, if you propose a new software to improve customer service, implement it in one department first. Collect feedback, adjust functionalities, and demonstrate improved customer satisfaction and team efficiency. With successful results in hand, pitching the software's adoption company-wide becomes a compelling narrative supported by data and real user testimonials.

In your march towards career advancement, let creativity and innovation be your banners. Not only do they make your professional journey more exciting, but they also carve paths to new opportunities and challenges. Remember, in a world that constantly evolves, those who innovate, lead. So go ahead, paint your career canvas with bold strokes of creativity and innovation, and watch as it transforms from being just another landscape to a masterpiece of professional success.

8.5 Leadership Skills for Aspiring Executives

Imagine stepping into a role where every decision you make not only affects your career trajectory but also the lives and careers of others. That's the daily reality for effective leaders. Leadership isn't just about guiding others; it's about inspiring them, making tough calls with a blend of courage and consideration, and steering projects to success against all odds. So, what does it take to not just manage but truly lead in the corporate world?

First off, being a visionary isn't about seeing the future with a crystal ball, but about having a clear picture of what you want to achieve and why. It's about painting this vision so vividly that others can see it too and are inspired to follow it. Visionary leaders are the north stars of their teams, providing a consistent sense of direction amidst the chaos of daily tasks and challenges. They articulate a clear purpose that aligns with both the organization's goals and the team's aspirations, transforming routine work into part of a grand strategy.

Then there's integrity, the backbone of genuine leadership. This isn't just about honesty in communication, but also about consistency between your words and actions. Leaders with integrity are trusted because their teams know they will do the right thing, even when it's hard, even when no one is watching. This trust is foundational, as it fosters an environment where open communication and genuine feedback are the norms, not the exceptions.

Empathy in leadership goes beyond understanding team members' professional needs; it's about recognizing their personal struggles, ambitions, and even the unspoken things that might affect their performance. Empathetic leaders are adept at adjusting their approach based on the individual needs of their team members, which can mean the difference between someone burning out under pressure and someone who feels supported to overcome challenges.

Decisiveness rounds out the core qualities of an effective leader. In a world where the only constant is change, the ability to make quick, informed decisions is invaluable. This doesn't mean rushing without thinking but rather having the courage to make a call even when the outcome isn't guaranteed. It's about not letting indecision stall progress and being accountable for the paths chosen.

Developing these leadership qualities isn't an overnight feat but a continuous process. Engaging in mentorship, both as a mentor and a mentee, is a fantastic way to hone your leadership skills. As a mentee, you gain insights from experienced leaders who can provide guidance based on real-life scenarios. As a mentor, teaching others allows you to refine your understanding and approach, often clarifying your ideas and strategies as you articulate them.

Leading project teams offers a practical arena to apply your leadership skills. Each project presents unique challenges and learning opportunities, whether it's managing resources, navigating team dynamics, or meeting tight deadlines. These experiences are invaluable; they're like live training sessions where you get to test theories, make mistakes, learn and improve in real-time.

Continuous personal development is another non-negotiable for aspiring leaders. The landscape of business changes rapidly, and staying updated with the latest trends, technologies, and leadership methodologies is crucial. This might mean taking up relevant courses, attending workshops, or simply dedicating time each week to read the latest industry publications.

Navigating organizational politics is often seen as a murky part of professional life, but it doesn't have to be. Understanding the power dynamics within your organization can help you make more informed decisions and advocate more effectively for your projects and teams. It's about knowing who the key decision-makers are, what their priorities might be, and how your work aligns with the broader goals of the organization. Effective leaders use this understanding to navigate their teams to success, ensuring their projects get the necessary support and resources.

Building and leading teams require more than just people management skills; it requires an ability to inspire and motivate. Start by building a team culture that values transparency, hard work, and mutual respect. Set clear goals, provide the necessary resources, and let your team members take ownership of their roles. Recognize and reward their efforts, and provide constructive feedback that helps them grow. Most importantly, lead by example. Show your team what dedication, accountability, and passion look like in action.

In essence, stepping up as a leader means transforming vision into reality, making tough calls with integrity, understanding your team's needs, and navigating the complex maze of organizational politics with savvy and tact. It's about being the kind of leader who not only achieves goals but also earns the respect and loyalty of your team. So, take the reins, set your sights high, and lead with confidence and empathy. Your leadership journey isn't just about climbing the corporate ladder; it's about the legacy you build along the way.

8.6 Achieving Work-Life Balance: Realistic Strategies for Busy Professionals

Remember the days when leaving the office meant leaving work behind? Neither do I. In today's always-on digital age, the boundaries between work and personal life are not just blurred; they're practically non-existent. But fear not, achieving a semblance of work-life balance is not as mythical as unicorns, even for us busy professionals. It's about making smart, sometimes tough choices to ensure that both your career and personal life are not just surviving, but thriving.

Let's start with the modern definition of work-life balance. It's no longer about splitting hours evenly between your office and your home. Instead, it's about finding a rhythm that allows you to excel in your job while also enjoying time for personal growth and leisure. This balance is personal and fluid, shifting as your life and priorities evolve. For some, it might mean remote working to cut down on commute time; for others, it might be about having the flexibility to attend a child's midday school play and make up the work hours later. The goal is to create a blend where both aspects of your life complement rather than compete with each other.

Now, onto practical balancing techniques. Time management is your best friend here. Start by auditing how you spend your day. Identify time wasters and look for efficiencies. Maybe batch checking emails rather than responding in real-time can save chunks of your day, or perhaps delegating certain tasks can free up your schedule. It's also crucial to set aside time for non-work activities that enrich your life, be it a hobby, exercise, or spending time with loved ones. Think of these activities not as luxuries, but as essential components of your day that recharge and refresh you, making you more effective in your professional role.

Negotiating boundaries with your employer is another key aspect of achieving work-life balance. This might sound daunting, but remember, the rise of flexible work arrangements has opened up new dialogues between employees and employers. Be clear about what you need, whether it's flexible hours or the ability to work from home a couple of days a week. Approach this conversation with a plan that outlines how your proposed arrangement is beneficial for both parties. For example, highlight how remote work can lead to fewer interruptions, allowing you to focus on high-priority projects. Remember, the goal is to find a win-win solution that respects both your professional responsibilities and personal needs.

Technology, while a boon, can be a double-edged sword when it comes to work-life balance. On one hand, smartphones and cloud computing allow us the freedom to work from anywhere, which can be fantastic for flexibility. On the other hand, they can tether us to our jobs 24/7. Managing technology wisely is crucial. Set specific times when you will and won't check work messages. Use tech solutions that help rather than hinder your productivity, like tools that streamline communication or automate routine tasks. And most importantly, don't be afraid to unplug completely from time to time. Your emails will still be there after your child's soccer game or after your yoga class—promise.

As we wrap up this discussion on work-life balance, remember that it's about making intentional choices. It's about not letting work consume your life but integrating it in a way that leaves room for passion and play. It's about setting boundaries and using technology as a tool to serve you, not enslave you. Most importantly, it's about recognizing that you are at your best when there is harmony between your professional achievements and personal happiness.

Part 2 Conclusion

WOW! That was a lot right? Imagine putting all this into writing! I'm still amazed we did it!

We've reached the end of our journey together in "Nothing Changes When Nothing Changes," and I couldn't be more thrilled. This book is all about one simple, powerful truth: to see change in your life, you must embrace change. It's been a ride filled with personal stories, practical advice, and a lot of hard-earned wisdom. In Part 1, we dove deep into the why and how of change. We explored the importance of a positive mindset, the need for accountability, and the reality of obstacles like procrastination and impatience. I shared my journey and the lessons I've learned along the way, hoping to light a spark in you. Remember, change starts with recognizing the need for it and being willing to take that first step, no matter how small.

Part 2 was our action plan. We got into the nitty-gritty of building routines, setting SMART goals, and tackling procrastination head-on. We talked about improving communication, managing finances, and maintaining a work-life balance. Each chapter was packed with practical steps designed to help you make real, lasting changes. The key takeaways are simple: embrace change, stay positive and accountable, overcome obstacles, and most importantly, take action. Knowledge without action is useless. Apply what you've learned, take small steps, and watch the transformation unfold.

This book is more than just words on a page; it's a call to action. I wrote it to share the principles and strategies that have worked for me and countless others. Now, it's up to you. Embrace these ideas, put them into practice, and let them guide you to the success and fulfillment you seek. Remember, every small step counts. Whether you're just starting or well on your way, keep pushing forward. The power to change is within you, and I believe in your ability to make it happen. Thank you for taking this journey with me. Now, go out there and start making those changes. Your future self will thank you. Stay strong, stay positive, and keep hustling!

References

Morning Routines: 14 Ways Successful People Start The Day https://www.usemotion.com/blog/morning-routines

Making health habitual: the psychology of 'habit-formation' and ... https://www.ncbi.nlm.nih.gov/pmc/articles/PMC3505409/

Treating Procrastination Using Cognitive Behavior Therapy https://pubmed.ncbi.nlm.nih.gov/29530258/

Goal Setting Techniques: Ways To Effectively Set and ... https://www.nsls.org/goal-setting-techniques

Mental Toughness in Athletes: How to Develop Grit https://www.redbull.com/us-en/mental-toughness-athletes-grit

Effects of Mindfulness on Psychological Health: A Review ... https://www.ncbi.nlm.nih.gov/pmc/articles/PMC3679190/

9 tips for setting healthy boundaries — Calm Blog https://www.calm.com/blog/9-tips-for-setting-healthy-boundaries

Keys To Building Resilience For Personal And Professional Growth https://www.forbes.com/sites/jiawertz/2024/04/22/keys-to-building-resilience-for-personal-and-professional-growth/

Active Listening: Using Listening Skills to Coach Others | CCL https://www.ccl.org/articles/leading-effectively-articles/coaching-others-use-active-listening-skills/

Assertiveness Training - Fact Sheets - ABCT https://www.abct.org/fact-sheets/assertiveness-training/

5 Ways Body Language Impacts Leadership Results https://www.forbes.com/sites/carolkinseygoman/2018/08/26/5-ways-body-language-impacts-leadership-results/

Conflict Management - StatPearls https://www.ncbi.nlm.nih.gov/books/NBK470432/

Your Guide to How to Budget Money https://www.nerdwallet.com/article/finance/how-to-budget

How to Invest in Stocks: Quick-Start Guide for Beginners https://www.nerdwallet.com/article/investing/how-to-invest-in-stocks

How to Create Multiple Streams of Income | *City National Bank* https://www.cnb.com/personal-banking/insights/create-multiple-streams-of-income.html

10 Ways to Prepare for a Personal Financial Crisis https://www.investopedia.com/articles/pf/11/prepare-for-a-financial-crisis.asp

How to be More Productive by Using the "Eisenhower Box" https://jamesclear.com/eisenhower-box

How to Delegate Effectively: 9 Tips for Managers - HBS On-line https://on-line.hbs.edu/blog/post/how-to-delegate-effectively

Best Time Management Apps of 2024 https://www.verywellmind.com/best-time-management-apps-5116817

How To Do a Time Audit (With Actionable Steps) https://hubstaff.com/time-tracking/time-audit

How Lifelong Learning Benefits Your Mental Health https://www.transformationsnetwork.com/post/how-lifelong-learning-benefits-your-mental-health

To Improve Your Work Performance, Get Some Exercise https://hbr.org/2023/05/to-improve-your-work-performance-get-some-exercise

Poor Sleep Reduced Decision-Making https://medicine.wsu.edu/about/highlights/poor-sleep-reduced-decision-making/#:~:text=Poor%20Sleep%20Results%20in%20Reduced%20Decision%2DMaking%20Ability&text=While%20robust%20research%20literature%20has,decision%2Dmaking%20go%20beyond%20fatigue.

Exploring the therapeutic effects of yoga and its ability to ... https://www.ncbi.nlm.nih.gov/pmc/articles/PMC3193654/

Learn to Love Networking https://hbr.org/2016/05/learn-to-love-networking

How Mentorship Can Benefit Both the Mentor and the Mentee https://money.usnews.com/careers/articles/how-mentorship-can-benefit-both-the-mentor-and-the-mentee#:~:text=Mentorship%20Is%20a%20Win%2DWin,while%20passing%20along%20their%20knowledge.

3 crucial team dynamics driving high-performing teams https://slack.com/blog/collaboration/team-dynamics-high-performing-teams

Repair is the Secret Weapon of Emotionally Connected Couples https://www.gottman.com/blog/repair-secret-weapon-emotionally-connected-couples/

A New Approach to Building Your Personal Brand https://hbr.org/2023/05/a-new-approach-to-building-your-personal-brand

Important Steps To Take When Planning A Career Change https://www.forbes.com/sites/robinryan/2023/10/18/important-steps-to-take-when-planning-a-career-change/

Advanced Networking: Six Techniques for Maintaining Professional Momentum https://www.science.org/content/article/advanced-networking-six-techniques-maintaining-professional-momentum

70% Of Employers Say Creative Thinking Is Most In- ... https://www.forbes.com/sites/rachelwells/2024/01/28/70-of-employers-say-creative-thinking-is-most-in-demand-skill-in-2024/

www.ingramcontent.com/pod-product-compliance
Lightning Source LLC
Chambersburg PA
CBHW061155120626
46546CB00005B/2073